# STUFFINGS

# STUFFINGS

## 45 INTERNATIONAL RECIPES TO ENHANCE FISH, POULTRY, MEAT, VEGETABLES, AND FRUIT

CAROLE LALLI

PHOTOGRAPHY BY JERRY ORABONA

HarperCollinsPublishers

For Nina, whose palate is as sharp as her wit

ACKNOWLEDGMENTS

With gratitude once again to my editor and good friend, Susan Friedland, who offered many good ideas and much good advice; to Evie Righter, whose cheerfulness was exceeded only by her sound editorial judgments; to Joseph Rutt, for an elegant design; and to Jerry Orabona and Joanne Rubin, who turned words into pictures.

HarperCollins books may be purchased for educational, business, or sales promotional use. For information please write: Special Markets Department, HarperCollins Publishers, Inc., 10 East 53rd Street, New York, NY 10022.

FIRST EDITION

*Designed by Joseph Rutt and Laura Lindgren*

ISBN 0-06-757502-1

Printed in Hong Kong

97 98 99 00 01 ❖/HK 10 9 8 7 6 5 4 3 2 1

# Contents

# INTRODUCTION

When I was about twelve years old a friend invited me to lunch. We started with soup, canned cream of mushroom made with milk rather than just water, which telegraphed the epicurean bent the meal was taking. Nevertheless, nothing could have prepared me for the centerpiece, a tomato stuffed with chicken salad, to date possibly the most elegant dish ever set before me. There was some sort of green salad around it and a soft, warm roll. I realize now that my friend's mother had mimicked for us the kind of lunch ladies liked in the 1950s. What is most remarkable is how those most common elements—chicken salad, tomato, and greens, the makings of a most ordinary sandwich—could be so transformed simply by their rearrangement. There is an unmistakable charm about stuffed dishes.

There also is practicality. Some foods beg to be stuffed, their very shapes suggesting the hollow interiors waiting to be filled. Tomatoes, peppers, eggplants, fruit, poultry. Beyond that, the monotony of having few ingredients to fashion into meals surely has motivated some cooks. If the eggplant, swell as it is, is your most ubiquitous crop, dinner can be a real challenge. Scooping out the flesh, combining it with various other ingredients, and stuffing it back into the vacant shell opens up all sorts of possibilities.

Thrift also can be inspirational. More than one of the recipes in this collection evolved from having just a bit of this or that on hand; the tomatoes filled with risotto, for one, the chicken stuffed with polenta, for another. These dishes are in the manner of cultures other than our own, where leftovers still are widely disdained. For French and Italian cooks, the trick is to invent a new dish out of the old, not just present the same meal a second time. Sometimes Italians refer to these dishes as *rifatti*—made again—and many of the reincarnations are as loved as the first.

Much of the time, stuffing suggests Thanksgiving and turkey. Everyone prefers his family's version and thinks it is *very* special. I heard a story recently of a man who raved on and on about his mother's stuffing to the point that one of his friends called the woman up and begged for her secret. Needless to say, she used a famous packaged brand and embellished it not at all. This really is about the comfort of the familiar, of course; in a world full of occurrences none of us can control, it is important that some things never change. What is now my own family's annual version—there had been others—is included here. It's pretty good, but I suspect it became institutionalized whenever it was my oldest child became aware enough to connect the stuffing to the Thanksgiving ritual. Try it some time other than Thanksgiving; for that day, of course, you must make your own.

# FISH
### *and*
# SHELLFISH

# SOUTHWEST STUFFED RED SNAPPER

❖ ❖ ❖ ❖ ❖

ASK YOUR FISHMONGER TO REMOVE THE BONES BUT LEAVE THE HEAD AND TAIL ON FOR A PRETTY PRESENTATION. THIS IS GOOD WITH RICE FLAVORED WITH CUMIN AND TOMATOES AND A MILD SALSA. THE FISH ALSO CAN BE COOKED OVER CHARCOAL FOR ABOUT 10 MINUTES ON EACH SIDE.

❖ ❖ ❖ ❖ ❖

*½ pound chorizo*

*2 teaspoons olive oil*

*1 red bell pepper, cut into small dice (1 cup)*

*1½ cups crumbled corn bread*

*1 large scallion or 3 small, cleaned,*
     *trimmed, and minced*

*½ cup fresh cilantro leaves, chopped*

*One 3½- to 4-pound whole red snapper,*
     *boned and butterflied*

*P*reheat the oven to 425°F.

Remove the sausage from its casing and put the meat in a heavy skillet over medium heat. Cook, stirring and breaking up the sausage, until most of its fat has been released, about 5 minutes. Remove the sausage to paper towels to drain.

Pour off the fat from the skillet and return the pan to the heat. Add 1 teaspoon of the oil and the red pepper to the pan, and cook, stirring until the pepper is soft, about 5 minutes. Remove the skillet from the heat and stir in the corn bread, scallion, and cilantro, taking care not to break up the bread too much.

Open the fish up on the work surface and spoon the stuffing onto one side, leaving about 1 inch at the outer edge uncovered; close the fish. (If it seems necessary, the opening may be secured with 2 or 3 toothpicks, but the amount of stuffing should not be so much as to prevent the fish from closing.) Brush a baking sheet and the top side of the fish with the remaining teaspoon of oil. Bake the fish on the oiled baking sheet for 20 to 25 minutes, just until the flesh flakes when tested and is no longer opaque.

*Photograph on previous pages.*

# SALMON FILLED WITH FRESH ARTICHOKES

4 SERVINGS

THE ONLY CHALLENGE TO PREPARING THIS DISH IS TO SLICE THE ARTICHOKES AND OTHER FILLING INGREDIENTS VERY THIN. IF THEY ARE, ALL WILL FINISH COOKING IN THE SAME TIME, WITH THE FISH SUCCULENT AND JUST A BIT OF BITE LEFT IN THE ARTICHOKES. THE YELLOW TOMATO IS THE BEST CHOICE BECAUSE ITS LOW ACIDITY WILL NOT ALTER THE FLAVOR OF THE ARTICHOKES, BUT PLUM TOMATOES ARE A FINE SUBSTITUTE.

One 3-pound or two 1½-pound fresh whole fish (such as salmon, red snapper, or bluefish), cleaned and boned but with head and tail left on
1 lemon
2 globe artichokes
¼ cup extra-virgin olive oil
Salt and freshly ground black pepper
1 yellow tomato, or 2 or 3 firm but ripe plum tomatoes, very thinly sliced
1 large clove garlic, sliced paper thin
Leaves from a good-size branch of rosemary

Preheat the oven to 450°F.

Wash the fish carefully and pat it dry with paper towels; place towels in the cavity to absorb any excess moisture.

Cut the lemon in half, add the juice and lemon half to a bowl of cold water. Cut away the stem of the artichokes and tear away and discard the outside leaves until the very pale inner leaves are exposed. Trim the tops about 1½ inches above the bottom; cut away the rough edges of the bottom.

Cut the trimmed artichokes in half, then into quarters. Remove the chokes from the centers. Slice each quarter as thin as possible and drop the pieces into the lemon water. Squeeze the juice from the remaining lemon half into a bowl, add the olive oil and salt and pepper, and whisk to combine. Drain the artichokes and pat them dry with paper towels. Toss the artichoke slices in the lemon-oil mixture.

Open the fish up to lay flat on the work surface and remove the paper towels. Lay half the tomato slices on one side, overlapping them slightly; lay half the garlic slices over the tomato slices. With your hands or a slotted spoon, lift the artichoke slices, letting the excess lemon-oil mixture fall back into the bowl; spread the artichokes over the garlic in a thick layer. Place the remaining garlic slices, then the remaining tomato slices over the artichokes, sprinkle with the rosemary leaves and bring the other side of the fish over to cover the stuffing.

Lightly brush a baking sheet with some of the remaining lemon-oil mixture, place the filled fish on it, and brush the top with more of the mixture. Bake for about 30 minutes, until the flesh is no longer opaque when tested and the skin is browned.

# GRILLED STUFFED SWORDFISH

✦✦✦✦✦

4 APPETIZER SERVINGS OR 2 MAIN COURSES

SLICES OF TOMATOES OR CHERRY TOMA-
TOES, SWEET PEPPERS, WEDGES OF
LEMON, AND ADDITIONAL LEAVES OF
BASIL MAY BE ADDED TO THE SKEWERS. IF
SERVING AS A FIRST COURSE, PLATE ONE
OF THESE ROULADES WITH A BIT OF
ARUGULA LIGHTLY DRESSED WITH RICH
OLIVE OIL AND LEMON JUICE PER PERSON.

✦✦✦✦✦

*4 thin slices swordfish steak, about ¼ inch
thick (total weight 1 pound); plus
4 additional ounces swordfish for the
stuffing*

*4 to 6 large whole spinach leaves, stems
removed, blanched, and patted dry*

*½ cup plus 2 tablespoons dry unseasoned
bread crumbs*

*2 tablespoons freshly grated Parmigiano-
Reggiano cheese*

*1 tablespoon olive oil*

*1 tablespoon capers in wine vinegar,
drained*

*4 large fresh basil leaves*

*1 extra-large egg*

*Freshly ground black pepper*

*1 lemon, cut into wedges*

Prepare a charcoal fire or preheat a broiler.

Place the 4 slices of swordfish on a work surface and pat them dry. Top each steak with a blanched spinach leaf, trimmed to fit.

Cut the additional 4 ounces of swordfish into several pieces and place them in the bowl of a food processor; pulse several times to chop. Add the bread crumbs, cheese, 2 teaspoons of the olive oil, the capers, basil, egg, and pepper; process just enough to combine the ingredients into a mealy mixture; do not overprocess.

Divide the mixture among the slices of swordfish, placing it near the smallest end and leaving about a ½-inch border along the bottom and sides. Roll the slices up. Push in 2 skewers, one near each end of the rolls to hold them flat. Brush the rolls all over with the remaining teaspoon of oil. Place the skewers on the grill or under the broiler and cook for 4 to 5 minutes; turn and cook on the second side, about 6 minutes. The fish and stuffing should be just cooked through but should not be at all dry. Remove the skewers before serving the fish with the lemon wedges.

# EAST-WEST TROUT

❖❖❖❖❖

6 SERVINGS

THIS IS NICE SERVED ON A BED OF CELLO-
PHANE NOODLES TOSSED WITH FRESH
WATERCRESS OR SPINACH.

❖❖❖❖❖

*Six 10-ounce trout, cleaned and boned, but
   with heads and tails left on*

*3 carrots, peeled and finely julienned*

*1 tablespoon water*

*1 medium red bell pepper, trimmed, seeded,
   and finely julienned*

*1 jalapeño pepper, trimmed, seeded, and
   slivered*

*1 clove garlic, minced*

*3 scallions, trimmed and peeled, finely
   julienned*

*1/4 pound shiitake mushrooms (about
   5 large), stems removed; caps julienned*

*1/4 cup fresh cilantro leaves, roughly
   chopped*

*One 1-inch piece of fresh ginger, trimmed,
   peeled, and minced*

*2 teaspoons rice wine vinegar or white wine
   vinegar*

*1 tablespoon dark sesame oil*

*Flour for dredging the fish*

*1/4 cup light soy or other neutral-flavored
   vegetable oil*

*Wedges of lime and lemon for serving*

*R*inse the fish and pat them dry.

Place the carrots and water in a small skillet or microwave-proof dish, cover and place over medium-high heat or microwave on high for 1 minute. Add the peppers, garlic, and scallions and return to the heat for an additional minute, or until the vegetables are just softened.

Let the mixture cool slightly, then pat away excess moisture with paper towels; toss together with the mushrooms, cilantro, ginger, vinegar, and dark sesame oil. Divide the mixture among the trout, tucking it into the cavities; close the cavities with toothpicks.

Sprinkle flour on a piece of waxed paper and dredge the fish all over in it.

In a large heavy skillet (cast iron, if possible), warm the oil over medium-high heat. Carefully place the trout in the oil and cook until golden brown on one side; turn and cook on the second side, 6 to 7 minutes altogether. Do this in two batches if necessary. If the fish seem to be browning too quickly before they are cooked through, cover the pan briefly (about 1 minute) but do not overcook them. Transfer the trout to a platter, remove the toothpicks, and serve with wedges of lime and lemon.

*Photograph on previous pages.*

# STUFFED CALAMARI

✦ ✦ ✦ ✦ ✦

6 APPETIZER SERVINGS OR 2 TO 4 MAIN COURSES

SERVE THESE AS A FIRST COURSE ON A BED OF SPINACH SALAD OR OTHER GREENS OR AS A MAIN COURSE ACCOMPANIED BY PARSLIED RICE OR LINGUINE OR VERMICELLI IN A VERY LIGHT TOMATO SAUCE.

✦ ✦ ✦ ✦ ✦

6 medium (about 1½ pounds) squid, cleaned
¼ pound sea scallops
¼ pound medium shrimp, shelled
½ cup soft fresh bread crumbs
1 small shallot
½ teaspoon fresh thyme leaves
¼ cup chopped fresh Italian parsley leaves
1 tablespoon small capers, rinsed and drained
1 extra-large egg
Pinch salt and freshly ground white pepper
1 tablespoon olive oil
1 cup dry white wine
1 bay leaf

Rinse the squid and pat them dry. Remove the heads, cut away the tentacles, and discard the remaining head material. Set the cavities aside. Place the tentacles, scallops, and shrimp in the bowl of a food processor and pulse or turn the machine on and off 3 or 4 times. Add the remaining ingredients, except the olive oil, wine, and bay leaf, and process, again using the pulse button, to make a uniform mixture that is ground but not pureed.

Spoon about 2 teaspoons of the mixture into each squid cavity; do not overstuff them—the mixture will expand and the squid will shrink somewhat during cooking. Use a toothpick or short trussing pin to close the cavities.

Warm the olive oil over medium heat in a skillet just large enough to hold all the squid in one layer. Add the squid and turn them gently to brown lightly all over. Add the wine and the bay leaf, lower the heat, cover, and cook at a simmer, turning the squid 2 or 3 times, until they are tender when gently pricked with the tip of a sharp knife, 20 to 30 minutes. Add water to the pan as the squid cook if the wine evaporates before the end of the cooking time.

# STUFFED CRAB CAKES

❖❖❖❖❖

4 SERVINGS

SERVE WITH TOMATO OR PARSLIED RICE, A SALAD OF MÂCHE OR WATERCRESS, AND FRESH TOMATO OR TOMATILLA SALSA. WHETHER THEY ARE STUFFED OR NOT, IT IS WORTH FINDING THE FRESHEST LUMP CRAB MEAT FOR EXCELLENT CAKES, AND THEN NOT USING MORE BREAD CRUMBS THAN IS NECESSARY TO BIND THEM. FOR BEST RESULTS, CUT THE INGREDIENTS FOR THE STUFFING VERY FINELY. BROWN THE CRAB CAKES OVER HIGH HEAT AS QUICKLY AS POSSIBLE — REMEMBER THAT THE CRABMEAT IS ALREADY COOKED — SO THAT THE AVOCADO DOES NOT GET HEATED THROUGH.

❖❖❖❖❖

*1 pound fresh lump crab meat*

*2 tablespoons mayonnaise*

*1 teaspoon Dijon mustard*

*½ cup fresh bread crumbs*

*1 extra-large egg*

*Freshly ground white pepper*

*½ fresh ripe avocado, peeled*

*2 teaspoons fresh lemon juice*

*4 sun-dried tomatoes (not packed in oil)*

*2 scallions, white part only*

*About 20 cilantro leaves*

*1 teaspoon cumin powder*

*1 teaspoon bottled jalapeño pepper sauce*

*2 teaspoons unsalted butter*

*1 teaspoon olive oil*

*Lime wedges for serving*

*C*arefully pick over the crab meat and discard any cartilage. In a medium bowl, combine the crab meat, a tablespoon of the mayonnaise, the mustard, bread crumbs, egg, and white pepper without breaking up the crab meat more than is necessary. Place the bowl in the refrigerator.

Cut the avocado into small dice and toss gently with the lemon juice. Mince the sun-dried tomatoes and the scallions. Chop the cilantro leaves and add them with the remaining tablespoon of mayonnaise to the avocado with the cumin and pepper sauce; toss to combine. Add additional cumin and pepper sauce to taste.

Remove the crab-meat mixture from the refrigerator and divide it into 8 mounds; gently flatten 4 of the mounds, and place about a quarter of the avocado mixture in the center of each. Cover each filled crab cake with a remaining crab cake and press around the edges to seal. Place the crab cakes on a plate and return them to the refrigerator for an hour or more.

Heat the butter and oil in a large heavy skillet over medium-high heat. Place the crab cakes in the pan and brown them thoroughly, 3 to 4 minutes per side. Serve at once or at room temperature with the lime wedges.

# ROASTED CHICKEN
# WITH POLENTA STUFFING

❖ ❖ ❖ ❖ ❖

4 TO 6 SERVINGS

THIS IS ANOTHER DISH THAT EVOLVED THROUGH THE OPPORTUNITY OFFERED BY LEFTOVERS, IN THIS CASE POLENTA. THE STUFFING IS SIMPLE BUT THE POLENTA CUBES PICK UP FLAVOR FROM THE CHICKEN WITHOUT LOSING THEIR OWN CHARACTER.

❖ ❖ ❖ ❖ ❖

2 cups chicken broth

1 cup water

½ teaspoon salt

1 cup medium-grind cornmeal

2 tablespoons chopped fresh sage

1 tablespoon unsalted butter

1 tablespoon plus 1 teaspoon olive oil

1 medium onion, chopped

3 small inner ribs celery, leaves included, chopped

One 6- to 7-pound roasting chicken

In a large heavy saucepan, bring the broth and water to a low boil. Add the salt. Add the cornmeal to the broth and water very slowly, using your hand or a small measuring cup, stirring constantly, with a wooden spoon. Do not rush this process or you will have lumpy polenta. Cook the mixture slowly, stirring constantly until it is thick and forms heavy bubbles; when it is done, in 20 to 30 minutes, the polenta will easily fall away from the sides of the pan.

Pour the polenta into a 9- × 11-inch baking pan or a baking sheet with sides. Cool for 45 minutes to room temperature, then place in the refrigerator for at least 2 hours before continuing.

Preheat the oven to 450°F. Lightly oil a baking sheet. Cut the polenta into 1-inch cubes and place them, not touching, on the baking sheet. Place in the oven and bake, turning once, for 45 minutes, or until the cubes are toasted and somewhat dried.

Place the polenta cubes in a mixing bowl with the sage. Place the butter and a tablespoon of oil in a medium skillet over medium heat; add the onion and celery and sauté, stirring until they soften but do not brown, about 5 minutes. Fold the vegetables into the polenta and sage.

Wash and dry the chicken inside and out. Stuff the body and neck cavities with the polenta mixture; do not overstuff and do not break up the polenta.

Rub the chicken with the remaining teaspoon of oil and place it on a rack in a roasting pan. Roast for 15 minutes, then turn the temperature down to 425°F and continue roasting until it is golden brown and the juices from the leg joints run clear, about 1 hour longer. Let the chicken rest for 10 minutes before serving.

MICROWAVE METHOD FOR POLENTA

Place the cornmeal and the salt in a large bowl. Pour in the liquid while stirring. Cover the bowl with a plate and place it in a microwave oven. Cook on high for 10 minutes. Remove the bowl and stir the contents (the polenta will have begun to thicken around the edges). Return the bowl to the oven and cook for 5 minutes more. Stir the contents again—the polenta may be completely thickened and cooked; if it is not, cook for an additional 5 minutes.

# CAPON WITH ITALIAN-STYLE SPINACH STUFFING

This dish was inspired by a recipe in *The Cooking of Parma* by Richard Sidoli. The stuffing has a rich flavor and a beautiful green color. The flavor of capon, which is a bit more emphatic than chicken, stands up nicely to this stuffing, but chicken can be used in its place.

One 6-pound capon or roasting chicken

2 pounds fresh spinach, or two 10-ounce packages frozen chopped spinach, defrosted

2 cups day-old peasant or other sturdy-textured white bread, cut into 1-inch cubes

1/4 cup chicken broth

2 teaspoons olive oil

1/4 pound pancetta, diced

1 small onion, minced

3 scallions, white part plus 2 inches green, cleaned and thinly sliced

2 ounces pignoli, lightly toasted (optional)

4 ounces mascarpone (see Note)

1/2 cup freshly grated Parmigiano-Reggiano cheese

2 eggs, lightly beaten

Salt and freshly ground black pepper

Rinse the capon under cold water and dry thoroughly inside and out; set aside. If using fresh spinach, trim away the stems, tough ribs, and any bruised or very tough leaves; wash the spinach thoroughly. Drain and place the spinach with any water clinging to its leaves in a large skillet with a lid. Place the skillet over medium-high heat, cover, and cook until the spinach is wilted, 1 minute. Turn the spinach into a colander and refresh under cold water; drain thoroughly.

If using frozen spinach, place it in a colander and press to remove as much water as possible. Place the frozen or fresh spinach on paper towels, roll up, and squeeze gently to remove any excess water. Chop the fresh spinach and set it aside.

Place the bread cubes in a large bowl and toss them with the chicken broth.

Place a small skillet or sauté pan over medium heat. Add 1 teaspoon of the olive oil and the pancetta and cook 3 to 5 minutes, stirring occasionally, until virtually all the fat has been rendered from the pancetta and it is nicely browned but not burned. Remove the pancetta to paper towels to drain.

Remove all but about 1 scant tablespoon of fat from the skillet and return the skillet to the heat. Add the onion to the skillet and cook, stirring, until it is soft and translucent, but not browned. Add the spinach to the skillet and combine and cook with the onion for about 2 minutes.

Preheat the oven to 450°F.

Add the spinach mixture, the pancetta, scallions, pignoli, cheeses, and eggs to the bread and toss gently to combine well. Season with salt and pepper.

Stuff the body as well as the neck cavity of the capon with the spinach mixture; do not overpack. Rub or brush the bird with the remaining teaspoon of olive oil. Place the capon on a rack in a roasting pan, and roast for 30 minutes. Lower the heat to 350°F and roast for about 2 hours longer, or until the skin is golden brown and the juices that run out of the leg joints are clear. Let the capon rest for 20 minutes before carving and serving.

*Note:* Mascarpone is a fresh Italian dairy product similar to cream cheese. It is available at Italian markets or other specialty food markets.

# GRILLED CHICKEN WITH HERBED RICOTTA UNDER THE SKIN

STUFFING CHICKEN UNDER THE SKIN BEFORE GRILLING (OR BROILING) IS A WONDERFUL WAY TO IMPART FLAVORS TO IT AND TO KEEP IT MOIST. THE METHOD IS NOT NEARLY SO HAIR-RAISING AS IT SOUNDS; THE SKIN IS SURPRISINGLY RESILIENT IF YOU ARE FIRM BUT CAREFUL. IT IS ADVANTAGEOUS TO PREPARE THE CHICKEN A FEW HOURS AHEAD OF TIME, IF POSSIBLE, AND THEN KEEP IT REFRIGERATED UNTIL ABOUT 15 MINUTES BEFORE YOU WISH TO COOK IT. THIS METHOD IS EXCELLENT FOR "BABY" CHICKENS— POUSSINS—OR CORNISH HENS. ALLOW HALF A BIRD TO A WHOLE PER PORTION, DEPENDING ON THE SIZE.

2/3 cup fresh ricotta

1 tablespoon unsalted butter, softened

2 tablespoons grated Parmigiano-Reggiano cheese

10 to 12 large basil leaves, chopped

1 small clove garlic, minced

One 3- to 3½-pound broiler, butterflied or split, washed under cold water, and dried

1 teaspoon olive oil

*P*repare a charcoal grill or preheat a broiler.

Combine all the ingredients except the chicken and olive oil in a small bowl. Lay the chicken, cut side down, on a work surface. Working from any side of the chicken, gently separate the skin from the flesh. Push small amounts of the stuffing between the skin and flesh and press gently from the skin side to move it in and to distribute it evenly along the surface of the flesh. Try not to tear the skin, but even a small tear will not mean disaster.

Carefully brush the oil all over the chicken.

When the coals are covered with white ash, place the chicken, bone side down, on the grill. Cook until golden brown; use tongs, or other utensils that will not cut the skin, to very carefully turn the chicken. Grill on the skin side until the skin is golden brown and the juices from the leg joints run clear, 10 to 15 minutes per side. Let the chicken rest for a few minutes before cutting it into portions.

VARIATION: GOAT CHEESE AND SUN-DRIED TOMATO STUFFING
*6 ounces fresh goat cheese, softened*
*4 scallions, trimmed and cleaned, all but 1 inch green tops removed; thinly sliced*
*4 sun-dried tomatoes, minced*
*2 teaspoons minced fresh rosemary or thyme leaves*
*2 teaspoons olive oil*

Combine the ingredients thoroughly and follow the procedure above for stuffing and cooking the chicken.

# CHICKEN BREASTS STUFFED WITH ROASTED RED PEPPERS AND SWISS CHARD

❖❖❖❖❖

8 large leaves green or red chard, trimmed
    and washed
6 ounces Italian Taleggio cheese, coarsely
    grated
2 whole roasted red peppers, chopped
2 tablespoons extra-virgin olive oil
8 chicken cutlets (about 2½ pounds),
    pounded thin
1½ cups unseasoned dry bread crumbs
2 eggs
2 tablespoons cold water
¼ cup light olive oil or other vegetable oil

*P*reheat the oven to 350°F.

Place the chard in a small skillet with just the water clinging to its leaves, cover, and steam briefly, until it wilts, about 1 minute. Immediately put the leaves in a colander or strainer and refresh under cold water. Squeeze out the excess water and place the leaves between sheets of paper towels.

In a bowl, combine the cheese, peppers, and extra-virgin olive oil. Roughly chop the chard and add it to the mixture.

Place 4 of the cutlets on a work surface and divide the chard mixture among them, mounding it in the centers; cover with the remaining cutlets. With a kitchen mallet pound around the edges of the cutlets, to seal them.

Spread the bread crumbs out onto a sheet of waxed paper. In a wide shallow bowl or soup plate, lightly whisk the eggs with the cold water. Dip the cutlets into the egg, coating both sides, and letting the excess egg run back, then lightly but evenly coat them with the bread crumbs.

Heat the oil in a large heavy skillet, preferably cast iron. Place the cutlets in the hot oil and cook until well browned on both sides, about 7 minutes altogether. Transfer the browned cutlets to a baking sheet and bake them in the oven until they are cooked and heated through, about 10 minutes more. Serve at once.

A "CAESAR" VARIATION

1 cup large fresh bread crumbs, pan-toasted in garlic and olive oil
¼ cup roughly chopped fresh Italian parsley leaves
8 or more anchovies, chopped
Freshly ground black pepper
2 ounces Parmigiano-Reggiano cheese, shaved

Mix together the first four ingredients.

Divide the cheese shavings among 4 of the 8 chicken cutlets, layering the cheese evenly, then top each cutlet with an equal amount of the bread stuffing.

Finish the cutlets, brown, and bake them as directed above.

# TURKEY BREAST
## WITH RICH CHESTNUT STUFFING

6 TO 8 SERVINGS

THE WIDE AVAILABILITY OF TURKEY PARTS THROUGHOUT THE YEAR HAS MADE IT AN ACCESSIBLE AND VERSATILE MEAL; FROM CUTLETS TO THIGHS, ENDLESS DISHES ARE POSSIBLE. THIS ONE INCORPORATES TRADITIONAL TURKEY ACCOMPANIMENTS INTO THE STUFFING — IT WOULD BE A GOOD CHOICE FOR A SMALL THANKSGIVING GATHERING.

*½ pound whole chestnuts (about 24), shelled and skinned (see Note)*
*1½ cups chicken broth*
*1 bay leaf*
*10 ounces fresh Brussels sprouts*
*Salt and freshly ground black pepper*
*1 pound sweet Italian sausage with Parmigiano-Reggiano cheese and parsley (or plain), without casing*
*½ cup chopped fresh Italian parsley leaves*
*2 teaspoons fresh thyme leaves*
*2 thick slices good-quality white or "peasant" bread, cut into cubes and lightly toasted (about 2 cups)*
*One 6- to 7-pound boned turkey breast, fresh if possible, tied as a roast*
*1 tablespoon unsalted butter, softened*

Place the chestnuts in a small pot with 1 cup of the broth and the bay leaf. Bring to a simmer and cook until the chestnuts are tender but not falling apart, about 20 minutes. Drain and set aside.

Trim the stem end of the Brussels sprouts and remove any tough or yellowed outer leaves. Cut a cross in the bottom of each. Bring a medium pot of water to a boil, add a big pinch of salt, and drop in the sprouts. After the water returns to the boil, cook the sprouts for about 5 minutes—they should have barely begun to cook. Drain the sprouts in a colander and immediately refresh them under cold water; set them aside to drain.

Preheat the oven to 350°F.

Place a medium skillet over medium-high heat. Add the sausage meat to the skillet. Cook, stirring and breaking up the meat until it loses all its pink color, about 5 minutes. Remove the meat to paper towels.

Pat dry any excess moisture on the Brussels sprouts and place them with the chestnuts on a work surface. Using a large chef's knife, roughly chop the sprouts and chestnuts, then place them in a medium bowl. Add the sausage, parsley, thyme, and pepper and stir to combine. Fold in the cubes of bread. Moisten with as much of the remaining broth as necessary to produce a mixture that will just barely hold together without becoming soggy.

Fill the neck cavity and the body end of the turkey breast with the stuffing, pushing the mixture into the center as well as possible, which will depend on how the turkey has been closed and tied. Brush the skin with the butter and place the turkey on a rack in a roasting pan. Roast until the skin is golden brown and the juices run clear, about 1½ hours. Let the turkey rest for 15 minutes before serving.

*Note:* To shell and skin chestnuts, first make a cross in the shells on the flat side, then drop the chestnuts into boiling water. Boil for 2 minutes, then drain and cover the chestnuts with cool water. When they are cool enough to handle, remove the shells and as much of the underlying skin as you can manage with a small paring knife; do not be concerned about small bits of skin that remain in the crevices. Keep the unpeeled chestnuts in the water as you work.

# LALLI FAMILY
# THANKSGIVING TURKEY STUFFING

THIS RECIPE YIELDS ENOUGH STUFFING FOR A VERY LARGE BIRD—UP TO 24 POUNDS, WITH SOME EXTRA STUFFING TO BAKE SEPARATELY IN A SMALL CASSEROLE. YOU CAN CUT THE RECIPE IN HALF FOR A 12- TO 14-POUND TURKEY OR TO A THIRD FOR A CHICKEN. TWO APPLES, CUT INTO LARGE DICE, CAN BE SUBSTITUTED FOR THE CORN KERNELS.

*2 pounds unseasoned bulk sausage meat*
*1/2 cup unsalted butter*
*1 large onion, chopped*
*1 large shallot, minced*
*3 inner ribs celery, leaves included, diced*
*Kernels from 4 ears of corn*
*4 fresh sage leaves, chopped*
*2 teaspoons fresh thyme leaves*
*12 or so cups broken-up day-old corn bread*
*1 cup chopped fresh Italian parsley leaves*
*1 cup (or less) chicken broth*
*Salt and freshly ground black pepper*

In a large heavy skillet over medium-high heat, cook the sausage meat, breaking it up, until it loses its pink color, 5 to 7 minutes. Remove the sausage with a slotted spoon and set it aside on paper towels to drain. Pour off the fat from the skillet, but do not clean the pan. Return the skillet to the heat.

Turn the heat down to medium and add the butter to melt. Add the onion, shallot, and celery to the pan and cook, stirring, for 8 to 10 minutes, until they are soft but not browned; scrape up any of the sausage bits clinging to the bottom of the skillet. Add the corn, sage, and thyme leaves and cook for 1 minute. Set aside to cool for about 10 minutes.

Place the bread in a large bowl; add the ingredients of the skillet along with the parsley. Combine the ingredients into a rough mixture—do not overcombine or break up the bread more than is necessary. If the mixture seems very dry, add just enough chicken broth to hold it together loosely. Season with salt and pepper; it is unlikely that you will need salt, as the sausage may add enough.

Pack the stuffing into the body and neck cavities of the turkey; fill the bird well but do not overstuff it. Any extra stuffing can be placed into a lightly buttered or oiled shallow baking dish, covered loosely with foil, and baked along with the turkey during its last half hour of roasting. Roast the turkey according to your favorite method or the method I use, which comes from James Beard. It results in a gorgeous mahogany brown bird that is nice and juicy.

Melt a stick of sweet butter and let it cool to room temperature. Rinse a double thickness of cheesecloth, soak it in the butter, and drape it over the turkey. Roast the turkey at 350°F for 18 minutes per pound, but my birds have always been finished ahead of this formula. In any case, if the turkey seems a bit underdone in the joints but finished in the breast, it is far better to remove the legs and return them to the oven than to overcook the breast. I usually don't do any basting for the first 30 minutes, but then baste every 20 minutes or so as the pan juices collect. Baste right through the cheesecloth; it may seem at first that the cheesecloth is irreversibly stuck to the skin, but in fact it will separate after time and basting.

# Squab with
# Wild Rice—Mushroom Stuffing

❖❖❖❖❖

You will have enough filling for 4 squab or 1 small roasting chicken. Small game birds seem to practically demand wild rice and mushrooms as an accompaniment. Here, they are in the birds. Fresh squab and quail are now widely available in specialty markets and through butchers, thanks to growers on both coasts.

❖❖❖❖❖

4 fresh squab

2 cups cooked wild rice (1 cup raw)

4 or 5 dried porcini mushrooms

1/3 cup lukewarm water

1 tablespoon olive oil, plus additional for roasting

4 ounces pancetta, minced

2 tablespoons unsalted butter

2 shallots, minced

1/2 pound fresh cremini, shiitake, or white mushrooms, chopped

2 tablespoons fresh thyme leaves

1/4 cup chopped fresh Italian parsley leaves

Salt and freshly ground black pepper

Preheat the oven to 425°F.

Wash the squab under cold running water and dry with paper towels; stuff a piece of towel into the cavity of each bird to absorb excess water.

Place the cooked wild rice in a large bowl.

Break up the dried mushrooms, place them in a small bowl, and add the lukewarm water to cover.

Place a small heavy skillet over medium heat and add a teaspoon of the oil. Add the pancetta and cook, stirring from time to time, until it is browned all over and has given up most of its fat, 3 to 5 minutes. With a slotted spoon, remove the pancetta to a paper towel to drain and pour the fat from the skillet.

Return the skillet to the heat and add the remaining 2 teaspoons of oil and the butter. Add the shallots to the pan and cook, stirring, for a minute or two to soften them. Add the fresh mushrooms, raise the heat slightly, and cook, stirring, until the mushrooms are softened and most of the juices they exude have evaporated, about 5 minutes. Add the cooked mushrooms to the wild rice.

Drain the dried mushrooms, reserving the soaking liquid. Roughly chop the mushrooms and add them to the rice mixture along with the pancetta and herbs. Mix the ingredients together and season with salt and pepper. Add a tablespoon or two of the reserved mushroom soaking liquid to moisten the mixture and help to hold it together.

Remove the towels from the cavities of the squab. Pack the stuffing into the body and neck cavities; close the openings with trussing needles if desired. Lightly oil a small roasting pan or large cast-iron skillet. Place the squab in the pan and brush them with oil. Roast in the oven until the skin is nicely browned and the leg juices run clear, about 25 minutes. Let the birds sit for about 10 minutes before serving.

# CHICKEN SAUSAGE AND SHIITAKE STUFFING FOR SMALL BIRDS

THE PRODUCTS OF BRUCE AIDELLS, A SAUSAGE MAKER IN SAN FRANCISCO, CAN BE FOUND IN SPECIALTY MARKETS AND SOME SUPERMARKETS ALL OVER THE COUNTRY. HIS CHICKEN SAUSAGE WITH APPLES, WHICH IS FLAVORFUL IN SPITE OF BEING QUITE LEAN, WAS USED IN THE ORIGINAL VERSION OF THIS STUFFING— USE IT IF YOU CAN. IF YOU DO, THE APPLE MAY BE OMITTED OR REDUCED FROM THE RECIPE HERE. THIS IS DELICIOUS WITH SOFT OR GRILLED POLENTA.

❖ ❖ ❖ ❖ ❖

*4 fresh squab, or 8 fresh quail*

*1 tablespoon light olive or peanut oil*

*½ pound chicken sausage or ground chicken*

*1 thick slice good-quality white or "peasant" bread, diced and lightly toasted (about 1 cup)*

*2 tablespoons unsalted butter*

*2 small or 1 large shallot, minced*

*½ pound shiitake or white mushrooms, diced*

*1 small apple, peeled, cored, and diced*

*2 tablespoons toasted pignoli*

*2 teaspoons fresh thyme leaves*

*¼ cup (or more) chicken broth*

*8 fresh sage leaves*

*4 thin slices pancetta*

Preheat the oven to 425°F.

Wash the squab or quail under cold running water, pat them dry, and put paper towels into the cavities to absorb excess moisture.

Heat 1 teaspoon of the oil in a medium skillet over medium heat. Add the chicken sausage and cook it until it has lost its pink color, breaking it up in the pan. Remove the sausage to the bowl and add the bread.

Add 1 tablespoon of the butter and the shallots to the skillet and cook, stirring, until the shallots are soft but not colored. Add the mushrooms to the pan and cook until they are soft and most of the moisture they exude has evaporated. Add the mushrooms and shallots to the bread mixture.

Add the apple, pignoli, and thyme to the bread and toss to combine them well. Add enough chicken broth barely to hold the mixture together—do not let it become soggy.

Remove the paper toweling from the birds and fill the body and neck cavities with the stuffing; close with string or trussing needles.

Heat the remaining 2 teaspoons of oil and tablespoon of butter in a large heavy skillet over medium-high heat. Add the squab to the pan and brown them all over, taking care not to break their skin; don't be concerned if they do not brown evenly. Remove the squab to a rack in a roasting pan. Place 2 sage leaves over the breasts and cover each squab with a slice of pancetta, pressing it down slightly onto the skin. (If you are using quail, put 1 leaf and ½ slice pancetta on each.)

Roast the squab for about 20 minutes—they should be nicely browned all over with the faintest pink in the juices that run from the leg joint. Remove the trussing needles and arrange on a heated platter for serving.

*Photograph on pages 12–13.*

# Barley, Turnip, and Fig
## Stuffing for Goose

❖ ❖ ❖ ❖ ❖

IN THIS METHOD THE GOOSE IS FIRST STEAMED ON THE STOVE BEFORE BRAISING AND ROASTING IN THE OVEN. THE RESULT IS A GOOSE WITH A NICE CRISP SKIN, TENDER JUICY FLESH, AND CONSIDERABLE LOSS OF FAT.

❖ ❖ ❖ ❖ ❖

*One 10- to 11-pound goose, innards, superficial fat inside, and wing tips (optional) removed*

*4 cups chicken broth*

*1 cup pearl barley*

*Salt and freshly ground pepper*

*3 medium turnips (about 1 pound), peeled, trimmed, and cut into ½-inch dice*

*4 leeks, tough outer layer and dark tops removed (cut just above the white part)*

*3 tablespoons olive oil*

*2 tablespoons unsalted butter*

*10 to 12 small dried figs, such as mission figs from California (½ pound; softened in water and drained if very hard)*

*Needles from 1 fresh branch of rosemary*

Rinse the goose thoroughly under cold water. Push skewers through the wings and legs to secure them. With another skewer, pierce the skin but not the flesh at the lower part of the breast and around the legs in several places, so the fat will drain during cooking. Place the goose on the rack of a roasting pan with a cover. Add 2 inches of cold water to the pan; bring the water to a boil over medium-high heat, cover the pan, then reduce the heat to a simmer. Steam the goose for 45 minutes to 1 hour, depending on its size; add more water as needed. Remove the goose from the pan and set aside to cool. Defat and reserve the cooking liquid.

Meanwhile, in a medium saucepan, bring the broth to a simmer over medium-high heat. Add the barley, and simmer, partially covered, until al dente, 12 to 15 minutes. Drain and refresh under cold water. Place in a large bowl.

Bring a pot of water to a boil. Add a large pinch of salt and the turnips, and cook them at a low boil, until they just give when pierced with a knife, about 5 minutes; do not overcook. Drain and refresh under cold water. Add to the barley.

Cut the trimmed leeks in half lengthwise and then crosswise into ½-inch pieces. Wash thoroughly under cold water and drain well. In a small skillet over low heat, cook the leeks, covered, in the oil and butter until soft, about 10 minutes. Add the figs and the rosemary to the leeks. Cover the pan and cook about 2 minutes longer. Add to the barley mixture and season with salt and pepper.

Preheat the oven to 325°F.

Remove the skewer from the goose's legs. Fill the neck and body cavities with the stuffing and replace the skewer. (Bake any excess stuffing in a small baking pan, covered, during the final 30 minutes of roasting.)

Measure the reserved cooking liquid. Add water or broth to measure 1 cup and pour into the roasting pan. Place the goose on the rack, cover the pan, and cook on the middle rack of the oven for 1 to 1½ hours, basting from time to time with the pan juices. The legs will move easily when the goose is nearly done.

Remove the cover and raise the oven temperature to 350°F. Roast and baste the goose until golden brown, 20 to 30 minutes longer. Place the goose on a platter, remove the skewers, and let it rest for about 15 minutes before carving.

# Meat

# SUSAN'S MOTHER'S STUFFED CABBAGE

❖❖❖❖❖

6 SERVINGS

IN CONVERSATIONS ABOUT RECIPES FOR THIS BOOK WITH MY FRIEND AND EDITOR, SUSAN FRIEDLAND, IT BECAME CLEAR THAT I HAD NO CHANCE OF DUPLICATING, LET ALONE EXCEEDING THE EXCELLENCE OF HER MOTHER'S STUFFED CABBAGE. SO WE HAVE INCLUDED IT WITHOUT MODIFICATION WITH MANY THANKS TO BERTHA GROSSMAN.

❖❖❖❖❖

*3 tablespoons margarine*

*½ cup coarsely chopped onion, plus 1 small onion, peeled*

*½ cup packed brown sugar*

*One 35-ounce can peeled tomatoes packed in tomato juice*

*2 cups tomato sauce*

*One 3-pound green cabbage*

*2 pounds ground beef*

*2 eggs, lightly beaten*

*¼ cup raw rice*

*2 tablespoons ketchup*

*Salt and freshly ground black pepper*

*½ pound pitted prunes (about 1½ cups)*

*½ cup raisins*

*Juice of 1 lemon*

In a large pot, melt the margarine. Add the chopped onion and sauté over medium heat for about 10 minutes, until it is soft and lightly colored. Add the brown sugar and stir with a wooden spoon, mashing out any lumps against the pot. Break up the tomatoes with your fingers and add them to the pot along with their juice and the tomato sauce. Cover the pot and simmer gently for about 1 hour.

Meanwhile, prepare the cabbage and the filling. Cut the core out of the cabbage and discard it. Place the cabbage in a large pot and cover it with boiling water. Put the lid on the pot and let the cabbage sit for about 15 minutes.

Place the meat in a bowl and grate the whole onion onto it. Add the eggs, rice, ketchup, and salt and pepper. Mix gently with your hands. If the mixture seems too dense and heavy, mix in up to ½ cup of warm water.

Remove the cabbage from the hot water. Peel off the leaves, one by one, without tearing them. If any leaves still seem stiff, put them back into the pot and bring the water to a boil. Remove the leaves after 2 or 3 minutes; they must be limp enough to fold without tearing. With a small sharp knife, shave off the hard ribs. Shred the center leaves which are too small to stuff and add them to the tomato sauce. Cut the large outermost leaves in half.

Place about ⅓ cup of the meat mixture into the center of each cabbage leaf. Fold the leaves so as to enclose the filling completely. One by one, place the stuffed cabbage leaves, seam side down, into the tomato sauce. Shape any leftover meat into meatballs and add them to the pot. Finally, add the prunes, raisins, and lemon juice. Cook over low heat, covered, for about 1½ hours.

*Note:* The cooked stuffed cabbage will keep in the refrigerator for several days and can be frozen for several months. Defrost before reheating.

# VEGETABLE-STUFFED MEAT LOAF

❖❖❖❖❖

6 TO 8 SERVINGS

IN THE 1950S, IT SEEMED AS THOUGH YOU COULD NEVER GET TOO MUCH PROTEIN, AND HARD-BOILED EGGS WERE THE STUFFING OF CHOICE FOR MEAT LOAF. THAT PASSION HAS GIVEN WAY TO AN EMPHASIS ON VEGETABLES, WHICH IS REFLECTED HERE. THESE ARE NOT JUST VEGETABLES, BUT VEGETABLES THAT REFLECT ANOTHER CURRENT TREND—ANYTHING MEDITERRANEAN. THE EGGPLANT AND THE GARLIC CAN BE ROASTED HOURS IN ADVANCE OF ASSEMBLING THE LOAF, BUT ARE BEST IF NOT REFRIGERATED.

❖❖❖❖❖

1 head garlic, plus 1 clove minced garlic

2 tablespoons olive oil

Pinch dried thyme

One 1-pound eggplant

2 pounds ground beef

1 pound ground pork

½ cup chopped fresh Italian parsley leaves

⅓ cup fresh bread crumbs

2 eggs

Salt and freshly ground black pepper

Several dashes bottled hot pepper sauce

3 roasted peppers

Leaves from 1 sprig fresh oregano or marjoram

*P*reheat the oven to 300°F.

Remove the papery outer skin from the head of garlic. Cut across the top of the bulb to expose just the tips of the cloves. Place the garlic in a small ovenproof dish, drizzle with a few drops of olive oil and top with the thyme. Double-wrap the entire dish in heavy-duty aluminum foil (or use a terra-cotta garlic roaster). Bake until the garlic is soft, slightly browned, and gives off a nutty fragrance, about 1¼ hours.

Raise the oven temperature to 400°F.

Cut the eggplant in half from top to bottom. Place a piece of heavy-duty foil over a baking sheet and coat it with some of the olive oil. Place the eggplant, cut side down, on the foil; brush the skin with more of the oil. Bake until the flesh is very soft and the skin is darkened and slightly shriveled, about 1 hour.

Lower the oven temperature to 350°F.

In a large bowl, combine well the meats, minced garlic, parsley, bread crumbs, eggs, salt, pepper, and hot pepper sauce.

Divide the meat loaf mixture into 2 unequal portions, one somewhat larger than the other. Place the larger amount on a baking sheet or shallow pan, pushing it up a bit at the edges to form an oval shallow well. Remove the skin from the eggplant and lay half the flesh in the well; cut the roasted peppers into thin strips and lay them over the eggplant. Pinch the roasted garlic out of its skin and place it randomly over the peppers with the oregano or marjoram leaves; cover with the remaining eggplant.

Shape the remaining meat into a rough oval about the size of the inner portion of the vegetable-filled bottom; place the oval over the vegetables and push the edges together to close them as well as possible. You will not be able to make a perfect seal, which is of no consequence.

Bake the meat loaf for about 1 hour, until its juices run clear; do not overcook or you will have a dry loaf.

CHUNKY THREE-TOMATO SAUCE

*1 tablespoon olive oil*

*1 scant pound (generous 2 cups) ripe cherry*
*    tomatoes*

*1 clove garlic, minced*

*1 tablespoon tomato paste*

*4 sun-dried tomatoes (not packed in oil),*
*    minced*

*6 leaves fresh oregano or marjoram*

*Salt and freshly ground black pepper*

While the meat loaf bakes, make the chunky three-tomato sauce: Place the olive oil and the tomatoes in a small saucepan over medium-high heat. Cook until the tomatoes begin to break down, about 10 minutes; add the garlic and cook for about 1 minute longer. Add the tomato paste, the sun-dried tomatoes, and oregano or marjoram, lower the heat, and simmer for about 15 minutes longer, until the cherry tomatoes are completely broken down and the flavors are incorporated. Season with salt and pepper. If the sauce seems too thick, add a few tablespoons of water to thin it to the desired consistency.

When the meat loaf is done, remove from the oven and let it rest for about 15 minutes. Serve with the chunky tomato sauce.

# BLACK-BEAN CHILI FLANK STEAK

*½ pound dried black beans, soaked in water
    to cover overnight*

*1 cup bottled Bloody Mary mix*

*2 cloves garlic, smashed*

*1 medium onion, cut into 6 or 8 pieces*

*1 bay leaf*

*2 to 3 sprigs fresh oregano, or 1 teaspoon
    dried*

*Freshly ground black pepper*


*1 clove garlic, minced*

*½ (or more) small hot pepper, seeds
    removed, minced*

*1 tablespoon dried oregano or marjoram*

*3 tablespoons olive oil*

*One 1½-pound beef flank steak, butterflied*

*1 small onion, chopped*

*½ cup corn kernels (1 ear)*

*1 teaspoon ground cumin*

*½ teaspoon chili powder*

*2 tablespoons red wine vinegar*

*1 tablespoon fresh oregano leaves, chopped*

*Salt*

*2 cups fresh plum tomatoes, seeded and
    roughly chopped (about 8 tomatoes)*

Drain the beans and place them in a medium pot with the Bloody Mary mix, the smashed garlic, onion pieces, bay leaf, sprigs of oregano, and a generous amount of black pepper. Add enough water to cover the beans by ½ inch. Place the pot over medium-high heat. As soon as the liquid begins to boil, lower the heat, cover the pot and simmer until the beans are quite tender but not mushy, about 40 minutes.

Meanwhile, mix together the minced garlic and hot pepper, dried oregano, and 1 tablespoon of the olive oil to make a paste. Open the flank steak up on a work surface and spread the cut surfaces with the paste. Place the steak between sheets of plastic wrap and set it aside.

Place 1 tablespoon of the remaining olive oil in a medium skillet over medium heat. Add the chopped onion and cook, stirring, until it is soft and barely browned. Add the corn kernels, cumin, and chili powder and cover the skillet for a minute or two to soften the corn slightly. Remove the skillet from the heat and stir in the vinegar, oregano leaves, and salt.

When the beans are cooked, drain them and refresh them under cold water. Discard the pieces of onion, the bay leaf, and oregano sprigs. Combine the beans with the corn mixture.

Lay the flank steak open on the work surface. Spread the bean mixture over the cut sides, topping the paste about ½ inch from the edges. Roll the meat up, starting from the narrowest end, snugly but not so much that the filling is pushed out. Tie the roll with kitchen or butcher's twine in 5 or 6 places.

Preheat the oven to 325°F.

Place the remaining tablespoon of oil in a large heavy skillet, preferably cast iron, over medium-high heat. Add the meat and brown it on all sides, turning it carefully with wooden spoons. Lay a double thickness of cheesecloth on the work surface and place the browned meat near one end. Roll the meat up in the cheesecloth and tie it snugly at each end, like a sausage.

Transfer the meat to a casserole that will just accommodate it, and spoon the tomatoes around it. Cover and bake for about 1½ hours, basting the meat

from time to time and turning it once. The meat should be tender when pierced with a sharp knife. Let the meat rest for about 10 minutes, then slice it into pieces about ¾ inch thick. Arrange the slices on a platter and spoon the pan sauce around them.

# CHEDDAR-STUFFED HAMBURGERS

❖❖❖❖❖

4 SERVINGS

EARLY ON, JAMES BEARD HAD THE GOOD IDEA OF TUCKING A BIT OF SOMETHING LIKE GORGONZOLA CHEESE INTO THE CENTER OF A HAMBURGER. ANOTHER SUGGESTION WAS A TABLESPOON OR SO OF FROZEN BUTTER THAT WOULD MELT WHILE THE BURGER COOKED AND DEFINITELY ADD TO THE JUICINESS. THE VERSION HERE IS LOWER IN FAT, BUT A DEFINITE INDULGENCE BECAUSE YOU NEED TO START WITH A SIZABLE BURGER FOR STUFFINGS TO MAKE SENSE.

❖❖❖❖❖

*1½ pounds best-quality ground beef*

*1 large clove garlic, chopped*

*½ cup chopped fresh Italian parsley leaves*

*¼ cup Dijon-type mustard*

*4 large white mushrooms*

*1 teaspoon olive oil*

*1 teaspoon unsalted butter*

*Salt and freshly ground black pepper*

*2 medium shallots, trimmed, peeled, and thinly sliced*

*2 ounces sharp Cheddar cheese, thinly sliced*

In a bowl, combine the meat with the garlic, half the parsley, and half the mustard.

Trim away the stems of the mushrooms and wipe the caps clean with a damp paper towel if necessary. Cut the caps into medium-thin slices. Place the oil and butter into a small skillet over medium-high heat. Add the mushrooms and cook, stirring, until they are lightly browned and most of the liquid they exude has evaporated. Remove the pan from the heat and season the mushrooms with salt and pepper. Stir in the remaining parsley and the shallots.

Divide the meat into 8 portions and pat them into thick disks. Spread the remaining mustard on 4 of the disks. Divide the cheese, then the mushrooms, and place on the mustard. Do not bring the filling ingredients to the edge of the disk. Cover each filled half with a remaining portion of meat and carefully pat the edges together.

Cook to your preference over a charcoal fire or on the stove in a heavy skillet.

# TOMASSO'S STUFFED VEAL BREAST

❖❖❖❖❖

12 SERVINGS

TOMASSO IS A RESTAURANT IN BROOKLYN, NEW YORK'S BAY RIDGE NEIGHBORHOOD. THE OWNER-CHEF, TOMASSO VERDILLO, TRAVELS OFTEN TO ITALY TO ADD TO HIS REPERTOIRE AND THE RESTAURANT'S REMARKABLE WINE LIST, BUT THE AUTHOR OF HIS STUFFED VEAL BREAST WAS HIS MOTHER, IDA.

❖❖❖❖❖

*1 or 2 loaves day-old Italian bread (1 pound)*
*1 cup milk*
*6 extra-large eggs*
*1 1/4 pounds ground veal or beef*
*1 cup cooked chopped spinach (can be frozen), well drained*
*1 pound ricotta cheese*
*1/4 pound grated Parmigiano-Reggiano cheese*
*4 cloves garlic, finely chopped*
*2 ounces pignoli, toasted*
*2 ounces white raisins*
*1/2 cup chopped fresh Italian parsley leaves*
*Salt and freshly ground pepper*
*One 7- to 8-pound veal breast, boned (bones reserved) with a pocket (see Note)*
*1 onion, sliced*
*1 to 2 cups veal or chicken stock*
*3/4 cup fresh or canned chopped tomatoes*
*1/2 cup dry white wine*

*P*reheat the oven to its highest temperature, 500°F or 550°F.

Roughly cut the bread into chunks and place it in a mixing bowl. Pour the milk over the bread and let it soak for about 15 minutes.

Break the eggs into a large mixing bowl and whisk them lightly. Add the ground veal, spinach, cheeses, and garlic and combine them well, using your hands if necessary. Squeeze the excess moisture from the bread, but keep it somewhat damp. Add the bread to the veal mixture. Fold in the pignoli, raisins, and parsley and season with salt and pepper.

Use the mixture to fill the pocket in the veal breast loosely (the mixture will expand considerably as it cooks). Sew the opening closed or secure it with trussing needles.

Place the roast on a rack in a roasting pan and place the pan in the oven to brown well, about 20 minutes. Once the veal has browned nicely, remove the pan from the oven and immediately turn the heat down to 275°F.

Scatter the onion and the reserved bones around the roast and pour in enough veal stock to barely cover the bottom of the pan; add the tomatoes and wine and cover with heavy-duty aluminum foil. Return the pan to the oven and roast the meat for 5 to 5 1/2 hours. Do not open the oven for at least 4 hours.

Remove the roast and let it rest for about 30 minutes. Meanwhile, pour off and de-fat any pan juices. Cut the roast into slices about 1 inch thick and place them on a serving platter; if the slices seem too broad for single portions, cut them in half. Spoon over a bit of the pan juices or pass them at the table.

*Note:* Ask the butcher for a veal breast for stuffing from an animal preferably milk fed and at least thirteen months old; otherwise you will get an inappropriately small cut of meat. Use the bones to make the stock called for in this recipe or roast them with the meat.

# VEAL INVOLTINI

❖❖❖❖❖

4 SERVINGS

Stuffed veal scaloppine too often are overcooked and feature bland fillings. Here the filling is savory and nicely textured; careful cooking will produce tender and juicy rolls. Serve them with buttered rice or orzo and steamed spinach.

❖❖❖❖❖

¼ *pound prosciutto*
¼ *pound Italian Fontina cheese*
*2 extra-large eggs*
*10 fresh Italian parsley leaves*
*2 to 4 fresh sage leaves*
*1½ cups dry unseasoned bread crumbs*
*2 cloves garlic*
*2 tablespoons olive oil*
*2 tablespoons pignoli*
*Salt and freshly ground white or black*
    *pepper*
*8 veal scaloppine, pounded*
*2 eggs*
*Lemon wedges for serving*

*P*repare a charcoal fire or preheat the broiler. Preheat the oven to 375°F.

Cut the prosciutto and the Fontina into a few large pieces and place them in the bowl of a food processor with the eggs, parsley, sage, ¾ cup of the bread crumbs, garlic, and 1 tablespoon of the olive oil. Turn the machine on and off a few times, or use the pulse button to produce an evenly chopped but not pureed mixture. Add the pignoli and pepper and process 1 or 2 times more.

Lay the scaloppine on a work surface and divide the filling among them, placing it along one end, leaving a ½-inch border on the sides. Roll up the scaloppine neatly.

Season the remaining bread crumbs with salt and pepper and spread them on a sheet of waxed paper. Break the eggs into a shallow bowl or soup plate and beat them lightly. Dip the involtini, one by one, into the egg, letting the excess fall back into the dish, and then coat them with the bread crumbs. Thread skewers through the involtini near each end, so they will stay flat. Drizzle some of the remaining oil over one side, place the rolls over the fire, oiled side down, and grill until nicely browned, about 2 minutes; drizzle the second side with oil, turn and grill until browned. If you are not using a charcoal fire, follow this procedure using the broiler.

Place the involtini in a baking dish just large enough to hold them. Bake until they are cooked through, about 15 minutes. Serve immediately with the lemon wedges.

# ROAST PORK STUFFED
# WITH GRILLED VEGETABLES

✦ ✦ ✦ ✦ ✦

6 SERVINGS

THIS IS A GOOD EXAMPLE OF THE
SERENDIPITOUS NATURE OF LEFTOVERS: A
SINGLE ROASTED PEPPER AND A SINGLE
SLICE OF GRILLED ONION FROM ONE SUM-
MER DINNER WERE INCORPORATED INTO
THE NEXT. AS WITH SO MANY DISHES
DEVISED FROM LEFTOVERS, THIS ONE
BECAME A FAVORITE. THE BEST WAY TO
COOK THE MEAT IS IN A KETTLE-TYPE
GRILL WITH THE COALS BANKED TO THE
SIDES AND THE GRILL COVERED, WHICH
PRODUCES AN INCREDIBLY SUCCULENT
ROAST AND IS FASTER THAN THE OVEN
METHOD. EITHER WAY, COOK THE BONES
ALONG WITH THE MEAT AND SERVE THEM
IF THE DINNER IS CASUAL, OR HOARD
THEM FOR YOURSELF.

✦ ✦ ✦ ✦ ✦

*1 red bell pepper, roasted*

*One 1-inch-thick slice of red or Vidalia*
*    onion, grilled or broiled*

*1 small clove garlic*

*1 tablespoon olive oil*

*1 teaspoon balsamic vinegar*

*Leaves from a 4- to 5-inch sprig fresh rosemary*

*Pinch crushed hot red pepper*

*Salt and freshly ground black pepper*

*One 4-pound boned loin of pork, tied, bones*
*    reserved*

*P*reheat the oven to 425°F.

Finely chop together the bell pepper, onion, and garlic; put the chopped ingredients in a small bowl and combine them with 2 teaspoons of the olive oil, the vinegar, rosemary, hot pepper, and salt and pepper.

Using a small knife, make a small opening in the center of the roast at each end. Using your fingers and a chopstick, push the chopped mixture through to the center at each end. Any leftover bits or juices can be spread over the roast. Rub the remaining oil over the roast and season with a generous amount of black pepper.

In a roasting pan, make a rack with the reserved pork bones and set the roast on it. Roast the pork loin for about 1 hour, until it is nicely browned and cooked through. Remove when the faintest touch of pink is just visible at the center; the meat will continue to cook for a few more minutes. Let the meat rest for 10 minutes before slicing.

*Photograph on previous pages.*

# LEG OF LAMB STUFFED WITH DRIED FRUITS AND BULGUR WHEAT

*1 cup chopped dried apricots*

*¼ cup dried currants*

*½ cup fresh orange juice*

*2 tablespoons balsamic vinegar*

*½ cup bulgur wheat*

*1 cup water*

*1 tablespoon olive oil*

*½ medium red onion, choppped*

*1 inch fresh ginger, peeled and finely minced*

*½ cup chopped fresh Italian parsley leaves*

*2 teaspoons fresh thyme leaves*

*1 boned and butterflied leg of lamb (about 4 pounds net weight)*

Place the apricots and currants in a medium bowl; add the orange juice and vinegar and enough hot water just to cover.

Combine the bulgur wheat, cup of water, and 2 teaspoons of the olive oil in a saucepan over medium heat. When the water comes to a boil, stir and cover; lower the heat to a simmer and cook until the water is absorbed and the wheat is fluffy, 10 to 15 minutes. Add the onion and remove the pan from the heat.

Drain the apricots and currants and return them to the bowl with the ginger, parsley, and thyme leaves. Add the wheat to the fruit mixture and stir to combine.

Preheat the oven to 425°F.

Wipe the lamb with paper towels and place it, cut side up, on a work surface. Spread the stuffing mixture evenly over the lamb, leaving about 1 inch uncovered around the edges. Roll the meat up, starting with the nearest end. The roll should be snug but not overly tight. Brush the entire surface of the meat with the remaining teaspoon of oil.

Tie the lamb crosswise with butcher's twine at 6 or 7 points. Put the lamb in a roasting pan, seam side down, and place it in the middle of the oven. Roast for about 1¼ hours for medium rare, or longer for more well-cooked meat. Let the roast rest for 10 to 15 minutes before cutting away the twine and slicing. Degrease the pan juices, warm them if necessary, and spoon them over the meat.

*Photograph on pages 28–29.*

# THREE-GRAIN SHIITAKE STUFFING FOR CROWN ROAST OF LAMB OR PORK

MAKES 8 CUPS STUFFING, ENOUGH FOR A 12-RIB CROWN ROAST

LAMB AND PORK—SPECTACULAR, RICH MEATS—CONTRAST NICELY WITH NUTTY GRAINS. THE DEPARTURE POINT FOR THIS RECIPE WAS THE THREE-GRAIN PILAF FROM THE WONDERFUL UNION SQUARE CAFE IN NEW YORK CITY. THE NUMBER OF RIBS AND THE NUMBER OF SERVINGS WILL CHANGE WITH THE MEAT; A LAMB ROAST WILL YIELD 12 RIBS AND SERVE 6 TO 7; A PORK ROAST, WHICH IS LARGER AND MEATIER, WILL ALSO HAVE 12 RIBS BUT SERVE 8 TO 10.

---

*1 tablespoon unsalted butter*

*1 tablespoon olive oil plus additional for roasting*

*1 cup wheat berries, soaked in water to cover for 2 hours*

*4 cups light chicken broth or a combination of broth and water*

*1 cup raw brown rice*

*1 cup smallest white beans, "rice" beans if possible (see Note), soaked in water to cover overnight*

*1 bay leaf*

*1 large clove garlic, smashed*

*P*lace half the butter and 1½ teaspoons of the oil in a large pot over medium-high heat. Drain the wheat berries and add them to the pot. Stir the wheat berries for a minute or two to coat them well; add 3 cups of the broth, bring it to a simmer, then lower the heat and simmer for about 30 minutes.

Stir the brown rice into the wheat berries and simmer for 20 to 30 minutes more, until the grains are tender but retain a bit of bite. In all likelihood, all the liquid will have been absorbed, but if it has not been, drain the mixture and set aside.

Meanwhile, drain the white beans and place them in a medium pot with the bay leaf, garlic, and black pepper. Add the remaining cup of broth and, if necessary, enough water to cover the beans by ½ inch. Place the pot over medium heat and when the liquid begins to simmer, lower the heat and simmer until the beans are tender, about 30 minutes. When the beans are cooked, drain and refresh them under cold water.

Break up the dried porcini, place them in a small bowl, and cover them with lukewarm water; let the porcini steep for about 10 minutes, then drain them, reserving the soaking liquid.

Place the remaining butter and 1½ teaspoons of oil in a medium skillet over medium heat. Add the shallots to the pan and cook them, stirring, for about 2 minutes; add the shiitake mushrooms and cook them until they have softened, 2 to 3 minutes.

Combine the wheat berries and rice, beans, and shiitake mushrooms in a large bowl. Chop the drained porcini and add them to the bowl, along with the scallions, parsley, and pecans, if using. Add a tablespoon or two of the reserved mushroom liquid, more if the mixture seems too dry, and season with salt and pepper.

*Salt and freshly gound black pepper*
*½ ounce dried porcini mushrooms*
*2 shallots, minced*
*1 pound fresh shiitake mushrooms, stems*
  *removed, diced*
*6 scallions, trimmed 1 inch above white*
  *portion and thinly sliced*
*½ cup chopped fresh Italian parsley leaves*
*½ cup chopped toasted pecans (optional)*

Preheat the oven to 350°F. Brush or rub the roast all over with olive oil. Place the roast, standing upright, in a shallow roasting or baking pan and place it in the oven. After 1 hour, spoon the stuffing into the cavity and cover it with a piece of aluminum foil to prevent it from drying out. Roast for about 15 minutes longer for lamb—the meat will be medium, still pink at the center. For more rare meat, add the stuffing after 45 minutes and roast for a total time of 1 hour.

For a pork roast, increase the initial roasting time by about 15 minutes for a total time of about 1½ hours. The meat should show palest pink at the center.

Let the roast rest for about 10 minutes, then, using a wide spatula, carefully place it on a platter. Discard the foil and carve the meat at the table, offering one or two ribs and a spoonful or two of stuffing to each guest.

*Note:* "Rice" beans are, as you might guess, small, though not quite as small as rice, and similarly shaped. They are beginning to appear in specialty markets and are worth seeking out, but other very small white beans, such as pea beans, will work equally well, though they may need a few more minutes of cooking time.

# VEGETABLES

# ARTICHOKES WITH
# PARSLEY-ANCHOVY STUFFING

❖❖❖❖❖

TOASTING THE BREAD AND MAKING LARGE CRUMBS KEEPS THE STUFFING FROM BECOMING SOGGY. THE AFFINITY OF PARSLEY AND ARTICHOKES IS EMPHASIZED, AND THE BALSAMIC VINEGAR ADDS A BRIGHT NOTE.

❖❖❖❖❖

*4 large globe artichokes*

*1 lemon*

*2 thick slices country-style white bread (not sourdough)*

*2 cloves garlic*

*2 to 4 anchovies packed in oil, drained*

*1 cup tightly packed fresh Italian parsley leaves*

*1 tablespoon fresh oregano, or ¼ teaspoon dried*

*Pinch crushed hot red pepper*

*4 to 5 tablespoons virgin olive oil*

*Salt and freshly ground black pepper*

*1 tablespoon balsamic vinegar (optional)*

*1 to 1½ cups chicken broth*

*C*ut off the stems and the spiky tops of the artichokes and trim the remaining leaves straight across with scissors. Spread the leaves open slightly and rinse the artichokes under cold running water. Cut the lemon in half and rub the artichokes all over with the cut lemon to keep them from discoloring. Turn the artichokes over on paper towels.

Toast the bread to color it lightly. When it is cool, break it into pieces and place it in the bowl of a food processor. Turn the machine on and off or use the pulse button to break the bread into large crumbs; remove the crumbs—you should have about 1½ cups.

Place the garlic, anchovies, parsley, oregano, and hot red pepper in the bowl of the processor and pulse to achieve a roughly textured mixture, adding 3 to 4 tablespoons of the olive oil—just enough to coat the ingredients lightly. Take care not to overprocess. Return the crumbs to the bowl and process just to combine. Season with salt and pepper and vinegar if desired (taste carefully, as the anchovies may add all the salt needed).

Place the artichokes on a work surface and carefully spread open the leaves. Distribute the stuffing mixture among the leaves, pushing the stuffing down lightly. Place the artichokes in a pan just large enough to accommodate them and pour the chicken broth and remaining olive oil into the bottom, to a depth of about 1 inch. Set the pan over medium heat; when the liquid begins to simmer, reduce the heat to maintain a low simmer, cover, and steam until a leaf comes away easily with a gentle tug, 30 to 45 minutes.

Remove the artichokes and set them on a serving dish; they will benefit from resting and should be served at room temperature. If there is considerable liquid remaining in the pan, raise the heat and cook the liquid down to about ¼ cup; spoon a teaspoon or so of the liquid over each artichoke.

# ROMAN SPRING ARTICHOKES

4 SERVINGS

THE STUFFING HERE REFLECTS LA VIGNAROLA, THE FABULOUS VEGETABLE STEW THAT IS ROME'S CELEBRATION OF THE PRODUCE THAT APPEARS IN MARKETS AT THE FIRST SIGN OF SPRING. FAVA BEANS, WHICH ARE INEVITABLY INCLUDED, HAVE BEEN OMITTED HERE BUT THEY CERTAINLY COULD BE SUBSTITUTED FOR ALL OR PART OF THE QUANTITY OF PEAS. THIS IS A PERFECT DISH TO START OFF AN EASTER OR PASSOVER DINNER.

*4 large globe artichokes*

*1 lemon*

*2 tablespoons unsalted butter*

*¾ cup chicken broth*

*2 thin leeks, trimmed and carefully washed*

*Salt and freshly ground white or black*
   *pepper*

*3 scallions*

*10 thin asparagus, washed*

*4 ounces fresh shelled peas*

*10 ounces fresh spinach, trimmed, washed,*
   *and roughly chopped*

*½ cup chopped fresh Italian parsley*

*½ cup grated Parmigiano-Reggiano cheese*

*¼ cup mascarpone*

Prepare the artichokes according to the method for Artichokes with Parsley-Anchovy Stuffing on page 48, reserving the stems. Trim the bottoms and outer portions of the stems, then cut the stems into matchsticks.

Push the leaves apart, pulling out those at the centers. Use a grapefruit spoon to remove the tough choke cleanly; you should have a cavity about 1 inch across.

Place the butter and the broth in a medium skillet with a lid. Cut the leeks about an inch above the white part, then in half from top to bottom and into ¼-inch pieces across. When the broth begins to simmer, add the leeks to the skillet with a pinch of salt and pepper, cover, and simmer for 5 minutes.

Trim the scallions about 2 inches above the white part and discard the tops. Cut the scallions crosswise into ½-inch pieces. Cut the asparagus into 1-inch pieces and add them to the skillet with the artichoke stems and the scallions, cover, and cook for 3 minutes. Add the peas and cook for 2 minutes. Add the spinach and cook it just until it is wilted, about 1 minute.

Drain the vegetables through a strainer placed over a pot that will hold all the artichokes, pressing gently to remove excess liquid. Place the vegetable mixture in a medium bowl with the parsley, half the Parmigiano, and the mascarpone; season with salt and pepper.

Fill the centers and some of the spaces between the outer leaves of each artichoke with the vegetable mixture. Place the artichokes into the pan over high heat; when the liquid begins to simmer, reduce the heat and cover the pan. Simmer until the artichokes are tender—a leaf will come out with just a gentle tug, about 30 minutes.

Preheat the broiler.

Remove the artichokes to a baking pan. Reduce the liquid remaining in the pot to about ½ cup and spoon it over the artichokes; sprinkle the remaining Parmigiano over the artichokes and run them under the broiler just long enough to brown the tops, about 5 minutes. Serve at once or at room temperature.

# STUFFED PORTOBELLO CAPS

INCLUDE THIS AS PART OF A VEGETABLE OR MIXED ANTIPASTI OR SERVE WITH SALAD GREENS.

*4 large Portobello mushrooms*
*½ cup fresh bread crumbs*
*1 clove garlic, minced*
*⅛ cup grated Parmigiano-Reggiano cheese*
*2 tablespoons pignoli, toasted (optional)*
*1 cup chopped fresh Italian parsley leaves*
*Salt and freshly ground black pepper*
*¼ cup (or less) olive oil*

*P*reheat the broiler.

Remove the stems from the mushrooms and wipe the caps with a damp paper towel if necessary.

Combine the remaining ingredients, adding just enough oil to moisten the mixture and hold it together, but not make it soggy. Divide the mixture among the mushroom caps.

Use any remaining oil to coat a baking sheet lightly. Place the filled caps on the baking sheet and place it under the broiler, about 6 inches below the heat. Broil until the mushrooms are cooked through and the top of the filling is toasty, 8 to 10 minutes. Serve hot or at room temperature.

# FILLED EGGPLANT WITH INDIAN FLAVORS

SERVE THESE WITH A SALAD FOR A HEARTY LUNCH OR LIGHT DINNER. FOR A FULLER MEAL, THEY ARE PERFECT TO ACCOMPANY GRILLED CHICKEN OR LAMB.

2 eggplants (about 1 pound each)
Salt and freshly ground black pepper
1 cup cooked rice (½ cup raw)
2 tablespoons olive oil, plus additional for
    the baking pan
1 small onion, chopped
2 cloves garlic, minced
1 small hot pepper, minced (optional)
2 to 3 medium tomatoes, or 8 plum
    tomatoes, seeded and roughly chopped
2 tablespoons dried currants
1 tablespoon curry powder
1 tablespoon ground cumin
2 tablespoons chopped fresh cilantro

Cut the eggplants in half from top to bottom. Using a small sharp knife and a grapefruit spoon, remove the flesh from the interiors, leaving a wall about ½ inch wide all around; take care not to cut through the skins. Salt the shells and turn them over onto paper towels. Roughly chop the flesh, toss it with a large pinch of salt, and let it drain in a colander.

Preheat the oven to 375°F. Place the cooked rice in a medium-large bowl.

Place the oil in a medium-size skillet over medium heat. Add the onion, garlic, and hot pepper, if using, and cook, stirring, until the vegetables are softened but not browned, about 10 minutes.

Raise the heat and add the tomatoes to the skillet. Cook, stirring, until much of the liquid has evaporated, 5 to 8 minutes. Add the mixture to the rice, stirring to combine.

Blot the eggplant flesh to remove as much moisture as possible and add it to the rice. Add the currants, curry powder, cumin, cilantro, and pepper and salt. Turn the eggplant shells over and wipe away any moisture. Divide the rice mixture among the shells.

Use the additional oil to coat lightly the skins of the eggplants and a shallow baking pan that will hold them without crowding. Loosely tent the pan with foil and bake the eggplants until they are cooked through—the skins will darken and begin to shrivel—and the tops are lightly browned, 30 to 45 minutes. If the tops have not browned, remove the foil, raise the heat to 400°F and bake for 5 minutes longer. Serve hot or at room temperature.

# FONTINA-FILLED ESCAROLE

❖❖❖❖❖

8 SERVINGS

❖❖❖❖❖

24 large escarole leaves, trimmed and
    washed (you may need 2 heads to yield
    enough large leaves; the inner leaves
    are good for salad)
1 teaspoon olive oil
1/4 pound pancetta, minced
1 clove garlic, minced
4 ounces Italian Fontina cheese, grated
4 tablespoons chopped fresh Italian parsley
    leaves
1/2 cup chicken broth
1 cup tiny cherry tomatoes or roughly
    chopped fresh tomatoes

*P*reheat the oven to 375°F.

Taking care not to break them, place the escarole leaves in a large skillet, cover and place over medium-high heat just long enough to wilt them, about 5 minutes. Carefully remove the leaves to a colander and refresh them under cold water. Place the leaves between sheets of paper towels to dry.

Place the oil in a small skillet over medium-high heat. Add the pancetta and cook, stirring, until it is browned and has given up most of its fat, about 5 minutes. Add the garlic and cook for about 1 minute longer. Remove from the heat.

Place the escarole leaves on a flat surface, overlapping and slightly fanning 3 leaves together to make 8 sets. Divide the pancetta, cheese, and parsley among the sets, placing them toward the root ends of the escarole. Roll up the leaves, tucking them in at the sides, to make cylinders.

Place the rolls, seam side down, in a baking pan large enough to hold them in one layer. Pour in the broth and scatter the tomatoes around the rolls. Tent the dish loosely with aluminum foil. Bake for about 1 hour, spooning the juices over the rolls once or twice. The tomatoes should have begun to split and collapse but still have some shape. Serve at once or while still warm with some of the juices spooned around.

# RADICCHIO STUFFED WITH
# PROSCIUTTO AND GORGONZOLA

THESE ARE SWOONINGLY DELICIOUS AND RIDICULOUSLY EASY TO PREPARE. THEY MAKE A GREAT FIRST COURSE WITH A BIT OF LIGHTLY DRESSED MESCLUN OR TOMATO SALAD TO THE SIDE. THE RESULTS OF COOKING THEM OVER CHARCOAL MAKE A FIRE WORTH THE TROUBLE. OF COURSE, IF YOU PLAN A GRILLED MAIN COURSE TO FOLLOW, IT MAKES EVEN MORE SENSE.

*16 large outer radicchio leaves*
*8 paper-thin slices prosciutto*
*6 ounces mascarpone or crème fraîche*
*6 ounces Gorgonzola, crumbled*
*2 ounces walnuts, toasted and chopped*
*1 tablespoon olive oil*

Prepare a charcoal fire or preheat a broiler.

Place the radicchio leaves on a work surface, putting 2 together, slightly overlapping, to make 8 sets. Lay 1 slice of prosciutto over each leaf, then divide the remaining ingredients, with the exception of the oil, among the leaves.

Starting from the root end, roll the leaves over the stuffing, tucking in the sides as you do. When the fire is ready, brush the rolls with the olive oil and place them on the grill, with the seam side down. Cook the roll for about 1 minute, until the leaves are softened and lightly charred, but not burned. Turn carefully with tongs and grill on the top side until lightly charred. Remove to individual plates, allowing 2 per serving, and serve at once.

# BAKED STUFFED ONIONS

✦✦✦✦✦

4 SERVINGS

LIKE MOST PEOPLE OF A CERTAIN AGE IN THIS COUNTRY, MY PRINCIPAL COOKING TEACHER WAS JULIA CHILD, THROUGH BOOKS AND OVER THE AIR. THE METHOD FOR PREPARING THE ONIONS FOR BAKING IS HERS AND IS TYPICALLY RESULTS-ORIENTED: THE ONIONS GET COOKED THROUGH WITHOUT BECOMING OVERLY TOUGH OR COOKED TO DEATH.

✦✦✦✦✦

*4 large (½-pound) sweet onions, such as
    Vidalia or red onions*
*Salt and freshly ground black pepper*
*2 links sweet Italian sausage (about
    ½ pound)*
*1 cup fresh bread crumbs*
*½ cup grated Parmigiano-Reggiano cheese*
*Approximately 1 cup chicken broth*

*B*ring a large pot of water to a boil. Trim the root ends of the onions, taking care not to cut into the layers themselves. Add a large pinch of salt to the boiling water, then drop in the onions and cook for exactly 1 minute. Use a slotted spoon to remove the onions from the water and cool them under cold water. Trim away the skins and cut across the tops to even them. Using a melon baller, hollow out the centers, leaving a generous cavity about 1½ inches across. Return the onions to the water, lower the heat, and simmer them gently for 10 to 15 minutes, until they are tender but still hold their shape.

Preheat the oven to 375°F.

Meanwhile, place a medium skillet over medium-high heat. Remove the sausage meat from their casings and cook, stirring and breaking it up, until it has lost all its pink color.

Place the sausage meat in a bowl with the bread crumbs and cheese and season with the pepper; it is unlikely that salt will be needed.

When the onions are cooked, refresh them under cold water and pat them dry with paper towels. Fill the cavities with the sausage mixture, mounding it over the tops of the onions. Place the onions in a baking dish just large enough to hold them, and pour the broth into the dish. Bake the onions, basting them with the broth several times, until they are tender when pierced with a sharp knife, about 1½ hours. Serve the onions hot or at room temperature.

# RED BELL PEPPERS
# WITH LENTILS AND SPINACH

❦❦❦❦❦

8 SERVINGS

SERVE THESE WITH GRILLED OR ROASTED LAMB, PORK, OR FISH OR WITH A SALAD AND BREAD FOR A SATISFYING LIGHT MEAL. THE FILLING ALSO CAN BE BAKED INSIDE TOMATOES.

❦❦❦❦❦

*1 cup green lentils*

*10 ounces fresh spinach, trimmed and*
*    cleaned*

*2 tablespoons olive oil, plus enough for the*
*    baking pan*

*1/2 cup diced carrots*

*1/2 cup washed and diced leek, white part*
*    only*

*1 small clove garlic, minced*

*1 tablespoon fresh thyme leaves*

*6 ounces fresh goat cheese*

*Salt and freshly ground black pepper*

*4 large red bell peppers*

*P*ick over and rinse the lentils. Bring a medium pot of water to a boil and add the lentils. Lower the heat and simmer until the lentils are just cooked, but not soft, about 20 minutes. Rinse and refresh the lentils under cold water. Turn the lentils into a bowl.

In a large pot or 10- to 12-inch skillet, steam the spinach just until the leaves are wilted. Drain and refresh under cold water. Squeeze all the excess water from the spinach and chop it coarsely; add the spinach to the lentils.

Preheat the oven to 375°F.

Heat the olive oil in a small skillet over medium-high heat. Add the carrots, leek, and garlic, and cook, stirring occasionally, until they are soft but not browned. Remove the pan from the heat and stir the vegetables into the lentil mixture along with the thyme. Crumble the cheese coarsely and add it to the mixture. Season with salt and pepper and additional thyme if necessary.

Cut the peppers in half from top to bottom. Trim the stem end and remove the seeds and veins inside. Divide the lentil mixture among the pepper shells.

Lightly oil a baking pan, and place the shells into it. Bake the peppers for 15 minutes, or until they are softened, but not collapsed, and the filling is hot. Serve warm or at room temperature.

*Photograph on pages 46–47.*

# BELL PEPPERS WITH ITALIAN BEANS AND SAUSAGE

❖❖❖❖❖

6 SERVINGS

THESE ARE SUBSTANTIAL ENOUGH TO BE A MAIN COURSE, WITH ONLY A SALAD AND BREAD NEEDED. THE BEANS CAN BE COOKED AHEAD TO SPEED UP THE PREPARATION. SIMPLY OMIT THE SAUSAGE FOR A MEATLESS MEAL.

❖❖❖❖❖

½ pound dried cannellini beans (or navy or pea beans or flageolets), soaked in water to cover overnight

2 cups chicken broth

1 tablespoon plus 1 teaspoon olive oil

2 cloves garlic

2 fresh sage leaves

About 6 large escarole leaves, trimmed and washed

½ pound Italian sweet or hot sausage links

4 ounces Italian Fontina cheese, diced

4 tablespoons fresh bread crumbs, from whole wheat country-type bread if possible

Salt and freshly ground black pepper

3 large, evenly shaped red or green bell peppers

*D*rain the beans and place them in a medium pot with the broth, 1 tablespoon of oil, the garlic, and sage leaves; add water to cover the beans by about ½ inch if necessary. Place the pot over medium-high heat and when it begins to boil, lower the heat and simmer gently until the beans are tender, 30 to 40 minutes.

Preheat the oven to 375°F.

Meanwhile, place the escarole leaves in a skillet, cover, and place over medium-high heat. Cook just to wilt the leaves. Turn the leaves into a colander and refresh them under cold water. Squeeze out as much water as you can and roll the leaves in paper towels.

Place a small skillet over medium heat. Remove the sausage meat from their casings and cook it in the skillet, breaking it up, until it has lost all its pink color. Remove the sausage meat to paper towels to drain.

When the beans are cooked, drain them and place them in a medium bowl. Roughly chop the escarole and add it to the bowl with the sausage, cheese, and bread crumbs. Season with salt and pepper; very little, if any, salt may be needed.

Cut the peppers in half from top to bottom. Trim the stem end and remove the sides and veins from inside. Divide the bean mixture among the peppers. Use the remaining oil to coat lightly the pepper skins and a baking dish that will accommodate the peppers in one layer. Bake until the peppers are tender and beginning to shrivel and the filling is browned on top, 25 to 35 minutes. Serve hot or at room temperature.

# BAKED POTATOES WITH WILD MUSHROOM STUFFING

✦✦✦✦✦

4 GENEROUS SERVINGS

THIS IS INSPIRED BY A RECIPE IN KATE RATLIFFE'S BOOK *A CULINARY JOURNEY IN GASCONY*, A CHARMING MEMOIR WITH RECIPES OF HER LIFE ON A CANAL BOAT IN FRANCE. THESE MAKE A GOOD FIRST COURSE, SERVED WITH WATERCRESS OR LAMB'S LETTUCE TO THE SIDE OR AS AN ACCOMPANIMENT TO GRILLED MEAT OR ROASTED CHICKEN.

✦✦✦✦✦

4 large, smooth, well-shaped baking
    potatoes, scrubbed but not peeled
Salt and freshly ground black pepper
2 tablespoons rendered duck fat or unsalted
    butter
1 tablespoon olive oil, plus enough for the
    baking pan
3 small shallots, minced
1 pound "wild" mushrooms (such as
    Portobello, shiitake, or cremini) or a
    mixture of wild varieties, or
    combination of white cultivated and
    wild, coarsely chopped
1/2 teaspoon fresh thyme leaves
2 fresh sage leaves, finely chopped
1/4 cup chopped fresh Italian parsley leaves
2 tablespoons heavy cream or crème fraîche
2 tablespoons grated Parmigiano-Reggiano
    cheese
1/4 teaspoon freshly grated nutmeg

Bring a large pot of water to a boil. At the long side of each potato, trim away a piece of about 1/4 inch; discard the small piece. Using a melon baller, remove the flesh inside the large piece of potato, leaving about 1/4 inch all around the edge to create shells; reserve the removed flesh.

Preheat the oven to 425°F.

When the water is at the boil, add salt to it and drop in the potato shells. Boil the shells over medium-high heat until they begin to become tender but still retain their shape, about 15 minutes. Remove the shells with a slotted spoon and let them drain, cut side down, on paper towels.

Meanwhile, roughly chop the reserved potato flesh. Put the duck fat into a medium heavy skillet over medium-high heat. Add the chopped potato and cook, stirring from time to time, until they are golden brown, 5 to 7 minutes; remove the potato with a slotted spoon to paper towels to drain. Set aside.

Lower the heat slightly and add the tablespoon of oil and the shallots to the skillet; cook them until they are soft but not browned, 3 minutes. Add the mushrooms and cook them, stirring, until they soften and much of the moisture they exude has evaporated, 5 to 7 minutes. Remove the skillet from the heat and stir in the herbs, cream, cheese, and nutmeg; season with salt and pepper.

If necessary, use a paper towel to dry up any moisture remaining in the potato shells and divide the mushroom mixture among them.

Lightly coat an ovenproof dish or baking pan with olive oil. Place the potatoes in the pan and bake them in the oven until the shells are completely cooked and the filling is bubbling and hot, 25 to 30 minutes. Raise the heat to 500°F, top the filling with the browned potato bits, and return the pan to the oven for 5 minutes or so to crisp the chopped potato topping. Serve immediately.

# BAKED SPINACH AND EGG POTATOES

❖❖❖❖❖

4 SERVINGS

THIS DISH GIVES NEW MEANING TO THE
NOTION OF HEARTY EATING. IT IS A MAR-
VELOUS BRUNCH OR LATE SUPPER DISH,
AN INDULGENCE AND A TRUE COMFORT.

❖❖❖❖❖

4 large baking potatoes, scrubbed
10 ounces fresh trimmed spinach, washed;
    or one 10-ounce package frozen
    chopped spinach, defrosted
2 tablespoons plus 1 teaspoon unsalted
    butter
½ cup grated Parmigiano-Reggiano cheese
½ cup grated French Gruyère
¼ teaspoon grated nutmeg
Salt and freshly ground white or black
    pepper
4 large or extra-large eggs

Preheat the oven to 425°F.

Bake the potatoes in the oven, right on the rack and *not* in aluminum foil, until they are cooked through, about 40 minutes.

While the potatoes are baking, steam the fresh spinach just long enough to wilt it. Refresh under cold water. Whichever type of spinach you are using, squeeze out all its excess water and wrap it in paper towels.

When the potatoes are ready, set them aside until they can be handled. Cut away about a third of the potatoes on one of the long sides—choose the side that is the least flat. Scoop the cooked flesh into a large bowl, leaving a shell of about ½ inch all around; take care not to break through the skin. Combine the potato with 2 tablespoons of the butter.

Chop the spinach and add it to the bowl. Combine the cheeses and add about ¾ cup to the bowl with the nutmeg and salt and pepper; combine well. Fill the potato shells with the spinach mixture.

Use the remaining teaspoon of butter to lightly coat a baking dish large enough to hold the potatoes; place the filled shells in the dish. Make deep wells in the potato mixture by pushing it to the sides. Carefully break 1 egg into each well and divide the remaining ¼ cup of cheese on top of them.

Bake the filled potatoes until the eggs are cooked to taste; they will need at least 20 more minutes for still-runny yolks. Serve at once.

# TOMATOES WITH BASIL-MOZZARELLA RISOTTO

❖ ❖ ❖ ❖ ❖

WITH THE ADDITION OF A TOSSED SALAD AND BREAD, THIS MAKES A SATISFYING SUMMER LUNCH. IT CAN ALSO BE USED AS A FIRST COURSE OR SIDE DISH TO GRILLED CHICKEN OR FISH STEAKS.

❖ ❖ ❖ ❖ ❖

*2 to 3 cups light chicken broth or a*
*    combination of broth and water*
*1 tablespoon unsalted butter*
*1 tablespoon plus 1 teaspoon olive oil and*
*    additional for the baking pan*
*1 medium shallot, minced*
*1 small clove garlic, minced*
*1 cup raw arborio rice*
*¼ cup dry white wine (optional)*
*6 large ripe tomatoes with no soft spots*
*Salt and freshly ground white pepper*
*1 cup loosely packed fresh basil leaves*
*½ cup grated Parmigiano-Reggiano cheese*
*1 cup cubed fresh whole milk mozzarella*

Bring the broth to a simmer in a small saucepan over medium heat. Lower the heat to keep the broth warm.

Place the butter and the tablespoon of oil in a medium saucepan over medium heat. Add the shallot and garlic and cook, stirring, for about 1 minute to soften but not brown them. Add the rice and stir to coat; the rice kernels will turn opaque with a white dot at their centers. Raise the heat slightly and add the wine, if using, to the pan. Cook the rice, stirring, until most of the wine has evaporated.

Turn the heat down to medium-low. Stir a scant ½ cup of warm broth into the rice. Cook, stirring, until most of the broth has been absorbed. Continue this process until the rice is tender but still somewhat firm to the bite (al dente); 20 to 30 minutes total. Take care not to overcook; the rice will cook further when the tomatoes are baked. Set the rice aside to cool to room temperature. The risotto may be prepared a few hours in advance, but should not be refrigerated.

Cut across the tomatoes about 1 inch from the top; reserve the tops. Carefully scoop out the flesh and seeds from the tomatoes into a strainer over a small bowl. Remove any sizable pieces of flesh and strain the juice into the bowl; discard the seeds. Salt the insides of the tomatoes lightly and turn them over onto a double thickness of paper towels. Roughly chop the tomato flesh.

When the risotto has cooled, roughly chop the basil. Stir in the cheeses, basil, chopped tomato, and 1 teaspoon olive oil. If the mixture seems thick and somewhat dry, add the reserved tomato juice by tablespoons. Season with salt and pepper.

Preheat the oven to 375°F. Lightly oil an ovenproof serving dish that will just accommodate the tomatoes. Use paper towels to absorb any excess moisture from the insides of the tomatoes. Wipe or brush the tomatoes lightly with olive oil.

Fill the tomato cavities generously with the risotto mixture, mounding it slightly; and cover with the reserved tomato tops. Bake the tomatoes for about 15 minutes, or until the mozzarella is soft and the filling is heated through. Serve warm or at room temperature.

# TOMATOES STUFFED WITH RICH MACARONI AND CHEESE

❖❖❖❖❖

6 TO 8 SERVINGS

THIS IS A TERRIFIC DISH TO PRECEDE A SIMPLE FISH OR POULTRY MAIN COURSE. AND, WHILE IT IS MARVELOUSLY CREAMY AND CHEESY, IT DOES NOT INVOLVE THE TRADITIONAL AMERICAN WHITE SAUCE BASE. THE BAKED MACARONI CAN ALSO BE MADE IN A CASSEROLE, WITHOUT TOMATOES.

❖❖❖❖❖

6 to 8 large firm ripe tomatoes
Salt
1 cup small elbow macaroni
¼ pound Italian Fontina, diced
¼ pound imported Gorgonzola, crumbled
2 tablespoons mascarpone or fresh cream cheese
2 tablespoons unsalted butter, in bits
¼ cup chopped fresh Italian parsley leaves
Freshly ground white pepper
2 tablespoons unseasoned dry bread crumbs
Olive oil for baking

Follow the method for hollowing and draining the tomatoes in the recipe for Tomatoes with Basil-Mozzarella Risotto (page 65).

Bring a medium pot of water to a boil; add a large pinch of salt and the macaroni, stir and cook for about 1 minute less than indicated on the box for al dente.

Preheat the oven to 375°F.

Meanwhile, in a bowl, combine the remaining ingredients, with the exception of the pepper and bread crumbs, stirring only enough to combine them. As soon as the macaroni is cooked, drain in a colander and refresh under cold water. Shake the colander vigorously to remove excess water, and return the pasta to the pan. Fold the cheese mixture into the pasta and season with the pepper.

Spoon the macaroni into the tomato shells, mounding it up a bit on the top. Sprinkle with the bread crumbs. Lightly oil a baking pan or dish just large enough to hold the tomatoes. Lightly oil the skins of the tomatoes and place them in the dish. Bake for about 20 minutes, until the tomatoes are cooked but not splitting, and the filling is bubbly and browned on top.

# TOMATOES WITH
# HERBED ZUCCHINI STUFFING

✦ ✦ ✦ ✦ ✦

✦ ✦ ✦ ✦ ✦

*4 large or 6 medium ripe tomatoes*

*Salt*

*4 slender zucchini*

*1 tablespoon olive oil*

*1 tablespoon unsalted butter*

*3 scallions, trimmed and thinly sliced*

*2 tablespoons heavy cream*

*1 cup cooked orzo or riso pasta (scant ½ cup raw)*

*¼ cup chopped fresh Italian parsley leaves*

*4 ounces Gruyère cheese, shredded*

*P*reheat the oven to 450°F.

Prepare the tomatoes according to the method for Tomatoes with Basil-Mozzarella Risotto (page 65).

Wash and trim the zucchini. Using the coarse side of a grater or an attachment for a food processor, shred the zucchini. Toss the zucchini with a large pinch of salt, and place them in a strainer or colander to drain for about 15 minutes.

Meanwhile, place 2 teaspoons of the oil and the butter in a medium skillet over medium heat. Add the scallions and cook, stirring, until they are soft but not browned, about 3 minutes.

Squeeze the excess moisture from the zucchini. Raise the heat under the skillet, add the zucchini, and cook, stirring, until much of the moisture has evaporated, about 5 minutes. Add the cream and cook briefly.

Turn the zucchini into a bowl, add the pasta, and toss to combine. Add the parsley and all but 1 generous tablespoon of the cheese. Brush or wipe the remaining oil to coat lightly the skins of the tomatoes and a baking dish just large enough to hold them. Sprinkle the remaining cheese over the filling.

Bake the tomatoes until they are cooked through but the skins are not splitting, and the tops are lightly browned, 15 to 20 minutes.

# STUFFED ZUCCHINI

❖ ❖ ❖ ❖ ❖

4 TO 6 SERVINGS

I MUST CONFESS THAT THE ZUCCHINI ITSELF IS NOT HIGH ON MY LIST OF FAVORITE VEGETABLES—THE FLOWERS ARE ANOTHER MATTER ALTOGETHER—BUT I DO LIKE THEM SHREDDED, A METHOD I LEARNED FROM *MASTERING THE ART OF FRENCH COOKING*, VOLUME 2. HERE, THE SHREDS ARE ENRICHED WITH EGGS, CHEESE, AND HERBS AND THEN STUFFED INTO HOLLOWED-OUT ZUCCHINI FOR A VERY EXCEPTIONAL DISH THAT CAN ACCOMPANY JUST ABOUT ANYTHING OR BE SERVED AS A FIRST COURSE.

❖ ❖ ❖ ❖ ❖

*12 medium zucchini, 2 inches in diameter
      at the widest point, cleaned*
*Salt and freshly ground black pepper*
*4 extra-large eggs, beaten lightly*
*¼ cup grated Parmigiano-Reggiano cheese*
*1 medium clove garlic, minced*
*1 medium shallot, minced*
*12 large basil leaves, chopped*
*¼ cup chopped fresh Italian parsley leaves*
*½ cup unseasoned, finely ground fresh
      bread crumbs*
*1 tablespoon olive oil*
*1 cup chicken broth*

Preheat the oven to 375°F.

Trim the ends of the zucchini, making sure that the broader ends are flat enough to stand up. Measuring from the bottom, cut the broad end of each zucchini into a 3-inch piece. Reserve the tops. Scoop out the pulp from the 3-inch pieces, leaving a ¼-inch wall all around.

Using the coarse side of a grater or an attachment for a food processor, shred the zucchini tops; you should have about 1½ cups. Toss the shredded zucchini with a large pinch of salt and place them in a strainer or colander to drain for about 15 minutes.

Squeeze the excess moisture from the zucchini and combine it with the eggs and cheese, then stir in the garlic, shallot, and herbs. Season with salt and pepper.

Fill the hollowed-out bottoms with the mixture and sprinkle them with the bread crumbs. Use the olive oil to coat a baking dish that will hold the zucchini comfortably. Place the zucchini in the dish, pour in the broth, and tent the dish loosely with aluminum foil.

Bake for 45 minutes, or until the zucchini give when gently pierced with the tip of a sharp knife. Remove the foil and bake for about 15 minutes longer to brown the tops. Serve hot or at room temperature.

# Desserts

# GINGERY BAKED APPLES

❖❖❖❖❖

4 SERVINGS

LOOK FOR GOOD, EMPHATICALLY FLA-
VORED GINGER SNAPS TO BRING SOME
SOPHISTICATION TO THIS FAMILIAR,
MUCH LOVED DISH. THE ONES I FOUND
WERE SMALL—ABOUT 1 INCH IN DIAME-
TER, AND DID NOT TURN MUSHY IN THE
BAKING.

❖❖❖❖❖

4 large baking apples
1/4 pound homemade or best-quality
    gingersnaps
2 tablespoons unsalted butter, plus
    additional for the baking dish
1/4 cup dried currants
2/3 cup applesauce
1 tablespoon dark rum
Lightly whipped cream or crème fraîche for
    serving

Preheat the oven to 375°F.

Cutting toward the center, at a slight angle, remove a piece from the top of each apple, about 1½ inches across. Carefully core the apples, increasing the space around the core to make a generous cavity.

Crush the gingersnaps in the bowl of a food processor, using the on/off or pulse button, but do not reduce them to powder. Add the butter and process just to combine. Stir in the currants.

Combine the applesauce and rum and add a tablespoon or more to the gingersnap mixture if it seems extremely stiff. Fill each apple with the gingersnap mixture, pushing the mixture into the cavity and mounding it at the top.

Lightly butter a baking dish just large enough to hold the apples; place the apples in the pan and spoon the applesauce mixture around them. Place the pan in the oven and bake for 30 to 40 minutes, until the apples are tender when pierced at the side with the tip of a sharp knife. Serve the apples warm or at room temperature on individual dessert plates with some of the sauce and the cream as an accompaniment.

# CORN CREPES WITH APPLE AND WALNUT FILLING

✦ ✦ ✦ ✦ ✦

8 TO 10 SERVINGS

FINELY GROUND CORNMEAL CAN BE SUB-
STITUTED FOR THE MASA HARINA IN THE
CREPES OR THEY CAN BE MADE WITH ALL-
PURPOSE FLOUR ONLY.

✦ ✦ ✦ ✦ ✦

## CREPE BATTER

*½ cup masa harina (see Note)*

*½ cup all-purpose flour*

*Pinch salt*

*1 tablespoon sugar*

*1 cup half-and-half or whole milk*

*½ cup water*

*5 tablespoons unsalted butter, melted and*
*    cooled*

*2 eggs*

*1 tablespoon dark rum*

*1 teaspoon vanilla*

*1 tablespoon soy or other neutral-flavored*
*    vegetable oil*

## FILLING

*½ cup raisins*

*½ cup warm apple juice*

*4 Granny Smith or other hard tart apples*

*2 tablespoons unsalted butter*

*¼ cup sugar*

*½ cup dark rum*

*½ cup toasted and chopped walnuts or*
*    pecans*

For the crepe batter: In a bowl, blend together the dry ingredients. Whisk in the half-and-half or milk and the water; add 4 tablespoons of the butter, the eggs, rum, and vanilla and whisk to blend well. Let the batter rest, covered, in the refrigerator for at least 2 hours.

When you are ready to make the crepes, check the consistency of the batter, which should be about as thick as heavy cream; if too thick, stir in a small amount of cold water.

Warm an 8-inch skillet over medium-high heat. Combine the remaining tablespoon of butter and the oil in a small bowl. Use a pastry brush to coat the bottom of the skillet lightly with the butter and oil mixture. Measure about ⅓ cup of batter into the skillet and swirl it around quickly so that it covers the pan in a thin layer. When the crepe bubbles up and is lightly browned on the bottom, turn it and cook it for just a few seconds on the other side. Slide the crepe onto a baking rack to cool. Continue making crepes with the remaining batter in the same manner; you should have 8 to 10 crepes. (The crepes can be made in advance, stacked between sheets of waxed paper, and stored in a plastic bag in the refrigerator for a few days or for a month or so in the freezer.)

For the filling: Place the raisins in a small bowl and add the apple juice. The raisins should just be covered; if they are not, add a bit more juice or water.

Peel and cut the apples into quarters; core them and cut each piece into 3 or 4 slices—they should be thin but not transparent. Warm the butter in a medium skillet over medium heat; add the apples and cook for 2 or 3 minutes, turning to coat them with the butter. When the apples begin to brown, add the sugar, turn up the heat, and continue to cook until the apples begin to caramelize. Add the rum, and ignite it while continuing to turn the apples, until most of the rum has been reduced and the flame has subsided, about 1 minute.

Drain the raisins, reserving the liquid. Off the heat, add the raisins and nuts to the apples. Add the reserved liquid by tablespoons if necessary to make a loose but not wet or mushy mixture. Let the apple filling cool to room temperature. (The filling can be made several hours in advance.)

*(continued)*

FINISHING THE CREPES
*1 teaspoon unsalted butter*
*¼ cup apricot preserves*
*Confectioners' sugar*
*Crème fraîche or lightly whipped heavy*
*cream for serving*

To finish the crepes: Preheat the oven to 375°F. Butter an ovenproof dish just large enough to hold the crepes snugly. Warm the preserves and strain them into a small bowl.

Lay the crepes out on a work surface and divide the filling among them, spooning it on the lower third of each. Roll the crepes up, folding in the sides. Arrange the filled crepes, seam side down, in the baking dish. Brush the top of each crepe with the apricot glaze. Bake the crepes for 10 to 15 minutes, until they are heated through and lightly glazed. Place 1 crepe on each dessert plate and sift the confectioners' sugar over it; serve at once with the crème fraîche or whipped cream.

*Note:* If you make crepes with masa harina or cornmeal in advance, you will have to reconstitute them in a covered skillet lightly coated with vegetable oil, much as you would with corn tortillas. If you use all-purpose flour, the crepes can be made in advance, returned to room temperature, and used as they are.

# AMARETTI PEARS

✦✦✦✦✦

PEARS AND ALMONDS ARE ONE OF THE CLASSIC COMBINATIONS IN DESSERT-MAKING. HERE IS ANOTHER MANIFESTATION OF THEIR AFFINITY.

✦✦✦✦✦

*½ cup whole almonds, preferably not blanched*

*12 amaretti cookies*

*¼ cup plus 2 tablespoons light brown sugar*

*2 navel oranges*

*1 cup fresh ricotta cheese*

*2 to 3 drops almond oil, or ¼ teaspoon almond extract*

*¼ teaspoon orange water or extract*

*8 Bosc or Anjou pears, ripe but not soft*

*1 tablespoon unsalted butter*

*Mascarpone, crème fraîche, lightly whipped cream, or softened vanilla ice cream for serving (optional)*

Preheat the oven to 350°F. Toast the almonds on a sheet of aluminum foil, turning them once or twice, for 10 minutes. Let cool.

Place the almonds, cookies, and the ¼ cup of sugar in the bowl of a food processor and process until the mixture is finely ground but not reduced to a paste. Grate the zest of one of the oranges and add it with the ricotta, almond oil, and orange water to the bowl; pulse 2 or 3 times just to blend.

Cut the tops off the pears at about the point that they become rounded; reserve the tops. Using a melon baller, scoop out the core and enlarge the cavity to about 2 inches across. Carefully trim any bumps from the bottoms of the pears that are preventing them from sitting squarely. Fill the cavities with the ricotta mixture, mounding it generously. Place the bottoms and the tops in a shallow baking dish that will just accommodate them without crowding.

Juice the oranges and pour the juice into the baking dish. Add the remaining 2 tablespoons of brown sugar, the butter, and, if necessary, enough water to bring the liquid about one-third of the way up the sides of the pears. Place the dish in the oven and bake the pears until they are tender when gently pierced with the tip of a sharp knife and the filling is lightly browned, 30 to 40 minutes; baste the sides of the pears—but not the filling—2 or 3 times during cooking.

Remove the pears and the tops to a serving dish or individual plates. Pour the cooking liquid into a small saucepan, place it over medium-high heat, and reduce the liquid to about ½ cup; it should be a thin syrup. Pour a tablespoon or so over the sides of the pears and either add the mascarpone or other garnish of choice to each plate, or pass it at the table.

*Photograph on pages 70–71.*

# MELONS FILLED WITH ROSY BERRIES

THIS MAY STRETCH THE CONCEPT OF "STUFFING," BUT IT IS A GOOD COMBINATION OF FLAVORS THAT MAKES FOR A LOVELY BRUNCH DISH. OR, ADD A PLATE OF SHORTBREAD COOKIES FOR A LIGHT SUMMER DESSERT.

*1 cup red raspberries, picked over and rinsed*
*¼ cup sugar, or less*
*Grated rind of 1 navel orange*
*2 tablespoons good-quality grappa, vodka,*
*    or balsamic vinegar*
*2 cups additional mixed berries (such as*
*    strawberries, blackberries, blueberries),*
*    picked over, washed, and trimmed as*
*    necessary*
*3 very small sweet, ripe melons (such as*
*    Galia or other very small melons)*
*6 sprigs fresh mint*

*P*lace half the raspberries in the bowl of a food processor or blender; add the sugar—less if the berries are quite sweet—and puree. Strain the mixture into a large bowl, and add the orange rind and grappa, vodka, or vinegar.

Fold the remaining raspberries and additional berries into the puree and set aside at room temperature for 1 to 2 hours before serving, or for up to 6 hours in the refrigerator. If you refrigerate the mixture, remove it at least 20 minutes before serving.

Cut the melons in half and cleanly scoop out the seeds. Taste the berry mixture for sweetness and adjust with additional sugar or grappa as necessary. Fill the cavities of the melons with the berry mixture and garnish with the mint sprigs. Serve in individual dessert bowls or on plates.

# CHOCOLATE-RASPBERRY ROLL

❖❖❖❖❖

8 TO 10 SERVINGS

A JELLY ROLL CAN HAVE MORE THAN
JUST JELLY, OR EVEN JAM, IN IT.

❖❖❖❖❖

## CAKE

*¼ cup cornstarch*
*⅓ cup all-purpose flour*
*¼ cup unsweetened cocoa*
*6 extra-large eggs*
*1 teaspoon vanilla extract*
*¼ cup chocolate-flavored liqueur (optional)*
*½ teaspoon salt*
*½ cup granulated sugar*
*Confectioners' sugar*

## FILLING

*1 cup heavy cream*
*8 ounces best-quality semisweet chocolate,*
  *shaved or finely chopped*
*8 ounces seedless or strained raspberry*
  *preserves*

## SERVING

*2 tablespoons unsweetened cocoa*
*Unsweetened whipped cream (optional)*
*½ pint fresh raspberries (optional)*

*P*reheat the oven to 375°F. Butter a jelly-roll pan (9 by 15 inches) and line it with waxed paper or parchment paper. Butter the paper and sprinkle it lightly with flour.

For the cake: Combine the cornstarch, flour, and cocoa and sift them together. Separate the eggs, placing the yolks and whites into medium bowls. Lightly beat the yolks with the vanilla and the chocolate liqueur, if using.

Beat the egg whites with the salt until the whites are foamy. Continue to beat, gradually adding the granulated sugar, until soft peaks form. Add about 1 cup of the whites to the yolks and stir to incorporate. Then add the mixture, along with the sifted dry ingredients, back into the whites. Fold the mixtures together thoroughly.

Pour the batter into the pan, leveling it with a metal spatula. Bake for about 15 minutes, or until the cake is lightly browned and a toothpick inserted into the center comes out clean.

Meanwhile, prepare the filling: Heat the cream until it just begins to show bubbles at the edge; do not let it boil. Place the chocolate in a small bowl and pour in the cream. Stir or gently whisk the mixture until the chocolate is melted and the mixture is smooth. Set aside to cool to room temperature.

Place a large, clean kitchen towel on a work surface. Sift the confectioners' sugar generously over the towel. When the cake is baked, remove it from the oven and turn it directly out onto the towel. Peel away the paper and trim the edges of the cake with a sharp knife.

Starting from the long side, roll the cake up in the towel, then unroll it. Let the cake rest for a few minutes, then roll it up again and let it cool.

When the cake is cool, unroll it and spread it with the raspberry preserves. Cover the preserves with the chocolate cream, spreading it evenly with a metal spatula to within ½ inch of the edges. Roll up the cake, again starting with a long side, and transfer it carefully, seam side down, to a serving platter.

To serve: Sift the cocoa over the top of the cake. Serve the roll with whipped cream and fresh raspberries, if desired.

# WALNUT-FILLED PUFF PASTRY POUCHES

✦✦✦✦✦

8 SERVINGS

Long before we became friends, I admired Mireille Johnston's book on the cooking of Provence, *The Cuisine of the Sun*. The filling here is hers, for a typical pie of the region. The pouches can also be made with phyllo dough. In any case, they are wonderful with crème anglaise or vanilla ice cream.

✦✦✦✦✦

*¾ cup sugar*

*¼ cup water*

*1½ cups chopped walnuts*

*6 tablespoons unsalted butter*

*½ cup milk*

*¼ cup honey*

*1½ pounds puff pastry (homemade or
    good-quality store-bought)*

*1 egg yolk, slightly beaten with 1 tablespoon
    milk or water*

*P*ut the sugar and water into a medium pan over medium-high heat. Cook, stirring, until the sugar melts, then simmer until the mixture begins to color lightly.

Off the heat, add the walnuts and the butter to the sugar syrup, stir, then add the milk. Return the pan to the heat and simmer for 20 minutes more. Stir in the honey, remove the pan from the heat, and let the mixture cool to room temperature.

Preheat the oven to 400°F.

Cut the puff pastry into 8 pieces. On a lightly floured surface, roll each piece into a 6-inch square. Cut a strip of pastry about ½ inch wide from one side of each square and reserve. If your kitchen is warm, place the squares in the refrigerator while you fill and shape each pouch.

Place about ⅓ cup of the walnut mixture at the center of each square. Gather up the pastry to make a pouch shape. Wrap one of the reserved strips of pastry around the neck of each pouch and "tie" it by bringing one end up and over the other.

Place the pouches on a baking sheet and brush them lightly with the egg yolk mixture, taking care not to let it fall onto the baking sheet. Place the sheet in the oven and bake until the pouches are evenly golden brown and nicely puffed, 20 to 25 minutes. Transfer the baking sheet to a rack and let the pouches cool. Serve the pouches slightly warm or at room temperature.

# METRIC CONVERSIONS

## LIQUID WEIGHTS

| U.S. Measurements | Metric Equivalents |
|---|---|
| ¼ teaspoon | 1.23 ml |
| ½ teaspoon | 2.5 ml |
| ¾ teaspoon | 3.7 ml |
| 1 teaspoon | 5 ml |
| 1 dessertspoon | 10 ml |
| 1 tablespoon (3 teaspoons) | 15 ml |
| 2 tablespoons (1 ounce) | 30 ml |
| ¼ cup | 60 ml |
| ⅓ cup | 80 ml |
| ½ cup | 120 ml |
| ⅔ cup | 160 ml |
| ¾ cup | 180 ml |
| 1 cup (8 ounces) | 240 ml |
| 2 cups (1 pint) | 480 ml |
| 3 cups | 720 ml |
| 4 cups (1 quart) | 1 liter |
| 4 quarts (1 gallon) | 3¾ liters |

## DRY WEIGHTS

| U.S. Measurements | Metric Equivalents |
|---|---|
| ¼ ounce | 7 grams |
| ⅓ ounce | 10 grams |
| ½ ounce | 14 grams |
| 1 ounce | 28 grams |
| 1½ ounces | 42 grams |
| 1¾ ounces | 50 grams |
| 2 ounces | 57 grams |
| 3 ounces | 85 grams |
| 3½ ounces | 100 grams |
| 4 ounces (¼ pound) | 114 grams |
| 6 ounces | 170 grams |
| 8 ounces (½ pound) | 227 grams |
| 9 ounces | 250 grams |
| 16 ounces (1 pound) | 464 grams |

## Temperatures

| Fahrenheit | Celsius Centigrade |
|---|---|
| 32°F (water freezes) | 0°C |
| 200°F | 95°C |
| 212°F (water boils) | 100°C |
| 250°F | 120°C |
| 275°F | 135°C |
| 300°F (slow oven) | 150°C |
| 325°F | 160°C |
| 350°F (moderate oven) | 175°C |
| 375°F | 190°C |
| 400°F (hot oven) | 205°C |
| 425°F | 220°C |
| 450°F (very hot oven) | 230°C |
| 475°F | 245°C |
| 500°F (extremely hot oven) | 260°C |

## Length

| U.S. Measurements | Metric Equivalents |
|---|---|
| ⅛ inch | 3 mm |
| ¼ inch | 6 mm |
| ⅜ inch | 1 cm |
| ½ inch | 1.2 cm |
| ¾ inch | 2 cm |
| 1 inch | 2.5 cm |
| 1¼ inches | 3.4 cm |
| 1½ inches | 3.7 cm |
| 2 inches | 5 cm |
| 3 inches | 7.5 cm |
| 4 inches | 10 cm |
| 5 inches | 12.5 cm |

## Approximate Equivalents

1 kilo is slightly more than 2 pounds

1 liter is slightly more than 1 quart

1 meter is slightly over 3 feet

1 centimeter is approximately ⅜ inch

# INDEX